WAR IMAGES

FABRICATING REALITY

Raphael Sassower and Louis Cicotello

LEXINGTON BOOKS

A division of
ROWMAN & LITTLEFIELD PUBLISHERS, INC.
Lanham • Boulder • New York • Toronto • Plymouth, UK

Published by Lexington Books
A division of Rowman & Littlefield Publishers, Inc.
A wholly owned subsidary of The Rowman & Littlefield Publishing Group,
Inc.
4501 Forbes Boulevard, Suite 200, Lanham, Maryland 20706
http://www.lexingtonbooks.com

Estover Road, Plymouth PL6 7PY, United Kingdom

British Library Cataloguing in Publication Information Available

Library of Congress Cataloging-in-Publication Data
Sassower, Raphael.
  War images : fabricating reality / Raphael Sassower and Louis Cicotello.
    p. cm.
  Includes bibliographical references and index.
  ISBN 978-0-7391-4310-0 (cloth : alk. paper) — ISBN 978-0-7391-4311-7
(pbk. : alk. paper) — ISBN 978-0-7391-3626-3 (eBook)
 1. War photography—History. 2. Images, Photographic—Influence—History.
3. Photojournalism—Political aspects—History. I. Cicotello, Louis, 1940- II.
Title.
  TR820.6.S27 2010
  779—dc22   2009045711

Printed in the United States of America

CONTENTS

PREFACE   vii

  1   MODERN AND POSTMODERN
      FABRICATION   1

  2   WAR IMAGES   25

  3   RECAPTURING REALITY   67

  4   THE PRAGMATIC PROMISE   93

BIBLIOGRAPHY   111

INDEX   115

ABOUT THE AUTHORS   119

PREFACE

To consider war images while the United States is engaged simultaneously in two wars as well as all the other wars and conflicts that rage around the world is to undertake a difficult task: no two wars are alike, and any generalization is bound to be partially wrong. Whether we agree with Heraclitus who quipped already in 500 BCE that "war is the father of all things," or with Carl von Clausewitz much later in 1832 that "war is nothing but the continuation of policy with other means," what is clear is that the specter of war is unfortunately permanent, and that therefore we should keenly observe its various manifestations. What we offer in this book acknowledges Richard Haass's view that in effect "all wars are fought three times. There is the political struggle over whether to go to war. There is the physical war itself. And then there is the struggle over different interpretations of what was accomplished and the lessons of it all" (Haass 2009, 216). Having been in the administrations of both presidents Bush, and currently as the president of the Council on Foreign Relations, his political experience warrants such an assessment. We believe that the three stages he outlines are more fully appreciated and more potently expressed through images rather than through logical arguments, rhetorical polemics, or with the aid of statistical data. The effectiveness of the visual language is such that it demands a careful and critical analysis, such as the one that we offer here. With all the nuances befitting war images, with all the sensitivity that should be accorded vanquished enemies and our own wounded and fallen soldiers, there is still much to debate and reconsider, to rethink and interpret. And we must keep in mind that the *experience of being at war* is much different from the experience of *viewing* a war image. Thus it is our *responsibility to engage war images critically and personally*, because lives are at stake and the future of world peace lies in the balance. Our own contribution is a necessary component that can challenge political manipulation and encourage public debate. The *iconic image* of any war and its ideological underpinning must be more fully appreciated.

War forces us to face our death and our inhumanity more so than any other experience. Soldiers die at war differently from the way citizens die in car accidents or because of a fatal illness: even when soldiers volunteer to fight, the war itself is always in principle preventable, unlike a disease or a freak accident. In the conduct of war, some of the great horrors of inhumanity are more pronounced than individual acts of cruelty or inappropriate group discrimination in peacetime. These generalizations can be contested, but for us they are important to emphasize from the outset of the book as a way to explain why we focus on war images rather than any other set of images worthy of analysis. Wars condone organized violence and rationalize certain modes of conduct that at peacetime would be condemned. As such, the traumatic experience of wartime wreaks havoc in the normalized and socialized psyche, breaking down an ordered psycho-social universe into a conflicted and fearful internal universe. The tension is felt personally and collectively, but expresses itself differently by those who participate in a war and those observing it from a distance. War images may seem to bridge the gap by providing visual references, but they simultaneously demonstrate that the gap can in fact never be bridged: active-duty soldiers and veterans respond to them differently than civilians. Is there a way to communicate across this divide?

In *The Golden Avant-Garde* (2000) we argued that what characterized avant-garde artists of the European-American axis throughout the twentieth century was their uncanny ability to walk a tight-line between complicity and criticism of the contemporary aesthetic and political establishment. Their balancing act has allowed them to gain great financial success in their respective cultures (and the status of celebrities, in some cases) while maintaining a respectable critical distance so as to allow them to challenge some features dominant among their fellow-artists. We labeled their cultural and professional position as *detached engagement*. This position allowed them simultaneously to be insiders and outsiders, mocking high-art as irrelevant to commercial art, while all the same accepting lucrative commissions and displaying their works in galleries and museums. Their artistic behavior may seem contradictory, or even hypocritical, until one realizes that it is the context and framework of their position that is more a reflection of their culture's own ambivalence about their role than their own insistence of being perceived as critics or obedient mouthpieces of their time.

Our exploration of the role of the avant-garde led us to consider, in our *Political Blind Spots* (2006), the underlying political and ideological foundation that inevitably informs artworks. Our claim there is that all artworks inevitably express some ideas or ideals, some values and norms that guide our cultures, even when these artworks are not overtly propaganda pieces. No artist is a cognitive or visual island and therefore is influenced by whatever social history and political reality that may surround the production of artworks. In this sense, one can *read* the ideology that informs a piece of art retrospectively, that is, backwards from the piece itself. Now in this process of *reading* one might find ideals not necessarily intended by the producers (artists and their political leaders). Yet, one can observe cross-culturally that there are some messages that are visually transmitted in what seems like a universal language of art: the same image is used by different nations to express the same idea, such as heroism, work ethics, family loyalty, patriotism, courage, and the like. The concern of misreading an image ends up being pedagogical in nature: can we teach our citizens to read images carefully and critically? Is there a way to disseminate ideas visually without encountering confusion and misunderstanding?

With these questions in mind we attempt here to deal with one particular set of images that convey ideas and illicit a response from viewers: war images. War images express more acutely than other images the kind of ideological principles we are interested in, because they end up dealing with death and suffering in the face of heroism and patriotism. It seems that pressing ideological differences express themselves more readily and are more explicitly challenged in declaring war on one's enemy. Our focus on images is also a concession to the fact that by the twenty-first century we live in an image-driven culture, where books and newsprint are becoming scarce if not obsolete, and where most knowledge claims are gathered and checked on the Internet (and not in class-rooms and libraries). We are still committed to the notion of *detached engagement* and the problems associated with *reading* the ideology underlying images, but we now refine our position: that consumers of war images must simultaneously pay attention to the details of any given image (and thereby uncover its ideology), while exploring other, alternative images related to the same war (search for multiple perspectives). Only in so doing can they avoid being led (or misled) down a particular interpretation that may turn out to be misleading. We shift, then, from *detached engagement* to *critical engagement*, one that is less ideologically driven and more *pragmatic*. The emphasis on the pragmatic reading of images has more to do with the power of images to convey, most commonly, a single idea or value, rather than to engage the observer with an inconsistent or contradictory set of ideas and values. This is where pastiche and collage come into play as compositional strategies through which many images are juxtaposed against each other so as to break the uniformity of an artwork, poster, or photograph.

The present recommendation may sound like an invitation to collect as many images as possible before one draws any conclusion about the justification of this or that war. It may sound as if we are saying that the more images are pulled together the less prone one is to overlook the *fabrication of reality*, by which we mean both the construction of reality and the lies and falsehoods that are intended in this construction. Yet, we are fully aware that simply having one hundred or one thousand images of our war in Iraq in and of itself is no guarantee against some misleading reading or misguided conclusion. Since the consumers of war images we are concerned with are not on the battlefield or even in the same country where the war is undertaken, they are bound to be limited to a fabricated aesthetic experience of remote reality. Because policy decisions in democratic societies are tied to public opinion, and public opinion is predominantly informed by images (in an image-driven culture), it stands to reason that we should be concerned about our interpretation of these images. We believe that outside of public debates over the legitimacy of any particular war the only *pragmatic* protection we can expect when personally experiencing war images is to set up simultaneous contrasting images: heroism and cruelty, victory and destruction, patriotism and barbarism, camaraderie and torture, prosperity and suffering. These contrasts highlight the inherent ambiguity that is characteristic of any war: there are costs associated with the decision to embark on one, and there are costs associated with carrying it out. Do the benefits outweigh the costs? Since there is never a simple answer to this and many related questions, we offer a *critical engagement* that is skeptical in nature and that refrains from adopting simple answers to complex questions. The discomfort we are going to feel when following this recommendation will force us to slow down from jumping into action in the case of declaring a war, and even when convinced that war is inevitable, we might be more cautious in exercising our power over others.

It would be reassuring and self-serving to imagine wars as ugly instances that we condemn, and to stereotype terrorists as dark-skinned hooligans wielding their weapons in public without any respect to civility and proper manners. Images like these would help us split the world between good and evil, between those in the right and those in the wrong, between *us* and *them*. But this black-and-white modernist demarcation no longer works in the postmodern realities of the twenty-first century (and perhaps never worked before). If wars aren't all quite grey, then they are definitely much more complex than we ever wanted to admit. Everyone is a bit in the right, and has some cause to fight for or against; and everyone is a bit in the wrong, using methods that are suspect and inappropriate in order to achieve laudable goals, such as world peace. This is how we have shifted from a modern to a postmodern world, one whose claims for legitimate acts of violence are publicly scrutinized. Only the extreme versions of religious fundamentalism (Christian, Muslim, Jewish, or other) are shielded from self-criticism, because they claim that the almighty speaks directly to chosen individuals who anoint themselves as spokesmen and all-powerful leaders (with bank accounts and armies, arrogance and indulgence, and in some cases cruelty).

With this in mind, it seems that the public consumes information and images, whether through print media, television newscasts, or the various websites on the Internet. In this book, we try to debunk the view that *modernist images of war and terrorism* lend themselves to an interpretation that is less complex: that there are good and bad guys, people worthy of hatred and killing, people against whom even a merciful God would declare war. Combat photojournalism is a perfect vehicle for this modernist version: transparent access to the realities of pain and suffering on the one hand (as justification for declaring war), and courage and sacrifice on the other (as justification for the conduct of war and a way to mobilize the public to pay for it). As we shall see in the rest of the book, every once in a while things get confused—when we fight a civil war and we have southern Confederates killing Yankees and vice versa—who are the good guys, after all? Judgments are made post-hoc, and generations of historians continue their debates about the American Civil War: no single image associated with this war allows for a definite interpretation.

The *postmodern condition* is one that acknowledges, just like the *human condition*, that life is too complex to be reduced to simple elements or variables, that humans are too interesting to turn into robots, and that ideas are too ambiguous and profound to be understood once and for all. There are always unintended consequences to our actions, inherent problems with the declaration of war or the designation of terror. Were the American colonialists terrorists or freedom fighters when they dumped tea into Boston Harbor and eventually declared their independence—claiming, like many others following their lead, *sovereignty?* Were American soldiers terrorists or freedom fighters when they slaughtered innocent Indian tribeswomen on their way westward, conquering millions of acres along the trail? Were the Bolsheviks terrorists or freedom fighters when they executed the Russian monarchy and aristocracy? These questions can be asked of any group of people around the globe who undertook to transform their countries and states in the name of an ideology. Any insurgency belies oppression and a dream of emancipation; any time humans are willing to sacrifice their lives for an ideal, they believe it to be worth their lives. Call them suicide bombers or martyrs, but their death and the destruction they bring about remains the same for those killed and hurt. So, should we retreat to a *relativist position* that says: well, it depends whose perspective you adopt, whose story you listen to? Or, should we claim that there is only one standard, one criterion according to which to make all judgments about war and terrorism?

In this book we try to trace this predicament visually: *analyzing the arguments underlying the emotional reactions we have to war images.* We don't endorse a *postmodern aesthetics* (however we try to define it by contrast to a *modernist aesthetics*), but rather illustrate the benefits and shortcomings of either visual approach to interpreting war images. This is important because war images are supposed to rally the troops and elicit public support for killing and suffering as much as they are supposed to prevent or end wars. The visual world that surrounds us is so powerful that wars are partially waged through them. But we must add that, psychologically speaking, even though we imagine that we can *simulate* if not completely *replicate* the experience of war with war images, this feat is a difficult undertaking. Though we don't directly engage films here, one can make the argument that films are composed of thousands of framed images that on their own would warrant the same analysis given here to still images. The aesthetic experience, however intense, is not a war experience, and the one could never substitute the other. The visual landscape itself is open to ideological manipulation—selection, framing, focus—so that we end up having to deal with theories and ideas even when we refuse to deal with them at first, for they end up determining and informing what images find their way into our cultural memory, that is, by being produced, distributed, and consumed.

Our hope for readers of this book is that they will become more *critically engaged* in reading war images, and that this engagement will provide them with the tools to argue for or against wars. When the German philosopher Immanuel Kant, for example, pleaded in 1779 for "perpetual peace," he provided a philosophical argument. When numerous political and religious leaders pleaded over the past century for world peace, they used common-sense and the threat of global annihilation. We believe that our plea for peace, temporary or permanent, can more fully resonate with a wide audience through careful and critical reading of war images. Our illustrations in this book are but a small sample of other war images that are available in libraries and on the Internet. We hope that readers will hone their visual reading skills here in a way that will serve them well in future critical readings of war images, or for that matter, in the critical assessments of any and all visual information.

*　　*　　*

We would like to thank Joseph Parry, our editor at Lexington Books, for having the confidence to publish this book and supplying all the technical support to secure permissions for image reproduction. We also would like to thank Ron Apgar, an artist, therapist, and a Vietnam War veteran, for his insightful comments on the psychological experience of war, and Sarah Martin and Drew Hutchinson, former students, who read drafts of this manuscript and provided useful comments for revision. Mandy Burch's assistance in producing the image files for the illustrations was invaluable. Our students over the past five years were thoughtful critics who demanded clear explanations for obscure references. As always, we thank our host institution for staying out of our intellectual way and allowing us to pursue our project unhindered. Part of chapter 4, section I, is loosely based on a previously published review by Raphael Sassower of George P. Fletcher and Jens David Ohlin's *Defending Humanity: When Force Is Justified and Why* (2008) in *Utopian Studies*.

Breckenridge and Colorado Springs, Colorado
June 2009

1

MODERN AND POSTMODERN FABRICATION

MODERN REALITY AND THE POSTMODERN CONDITION

Two basic assumptions guide us in this book: first, that by the twenty-first century we live in an image-driven culture, and second, that images are powerful instruments of cultural persuasion. The first assumption seems indisputable when examining the amount of money spent on advertisement, and the average number of hours that each citizen spends watching television. Our cell phones have become more meaningful communication tools with the advent of Facebook and other such websites because of the visual component they offer. We invest more money on our personal appearance than on our inner peace, and we have carried the slogan "one picture is worth a thousand words" to the extreme of using as few words as possible, both in our conversations and in our daily reading, since Twitter sound-bites rule the day, and since more daily newspapers around the country have closed or sought bankruptcy protection in 2009 than in the entire twentieth century.

Our second assumption is somewhat related to the first, insofar as it claims that the power of artworks is dependent on the dominance of visual culture. One of the advocates of such an assumption is Jacques Barzun who explains that, for him, the statement that "art is power" relies on the realization that "it influences the mind, the nerves, the feelings, the soul. . . . Art is deemed universally important because it helps men to live and to remember" (Barzun 1974, 21). Continuing along Barzun's lines of argument, we can observe the extent to which artworks, two-dimensional images and films, can both mollify and cultivate a sense of cultural belonging and loyalty to the political order, as well as foment the seeds of dissent with a revolutionary bravado unseen or expressed elsewhere; it is in this sense that art is indeed dangerous. It is important, then, to appreciate not only the power of art, but also the practical consequences of its influence, what it can do! According to Barzun:

> *Political*-revolutionary art is a logical and practical application of the discovery that art has the power to foment hatred of the world we live in. This power acts in two ways—by creating disgust through depicting what is and by creating hope through depicting a better life. Revolutionary salvation from the present may even be promoted by showing the actual as so abominable that any other state is to be preferred. (Ibid., 82–83)

The revolutionary potential for change is transmitted visually through images that depict what is to be abandoned and what is to be sought after. But this power of visual persuasion is dangerous as well, since it leaves in the hands of art producers—artists and their underwriters—the decision: what is to be condemned or condoned, what is bad and what is good. Since we are less interested in this book with art as an affirmation of life and its wonderful qualities (Ibid., 124), but rather with its role and particular powerful features in shaping our culture and its discontents, we remain focused on the criteria by which these distinctions are made. It is not simply a question of *who* controls images and in *whose* service they are produced (thus avoiding conspiracy theories), but more importantly a question about the conditions under which the *dissemination* or *distribution* of art allows for critical *consumption* of images. We believe that in order to answer this question we must appreciate the differences between modernity and postmodernity, not as historical periods but as approaches to the production, distribution, and consumption of art in general and of visual images in particular.

Modern philosophy is associated with the seventeenth century; modern art with the twentieth century; the Enlightenment period with the late eighteenth century; and so, the chronology of what we call modern aesthetic theory is fairly open-ended. By contrast, postmodern aesthetic theory is more easily associated with the late twentieth century and the beginning of this century. So, in terms of periodizaton, we are in a bind. Perhaps a more useful way of speaking about modern aesthetics is in terms of some characteristics that can be detected in this way of thinking across periods and time-lines. For example, modern art would be understood by some to capture the rational scaffolding that props up different styles and media, such that an explanation can be given to any analysis of visual presentation. To use the general Kantian schema, one employs criteria according to which aesthetic experiences are set aside from all other experiences. The Enlightenment leaders, put broadly, transformed the analysis of all human conduct from tradition and religion to a rational framework that allows one to set criteria and the conditions under which these criteria come into play. One's understanding could improve if one were free, says Kant, and if one had the freedom to use reason in public in all matters—in the Socratic dialectical manner or as critical reflection and analysis (Kant 1795/1983, 42). One should or should not own slaves not because God decreed so or because our ancestors always did so, but because it's immoral to treat people as a means rather than an end (Kant's ethics), or because it's less efficient from an economic standpoint, as some classical economists already understood in the eighteenth century (Adam Smith 1776, 37). There is "reason" behind the texture and content, frame and color, and the reason or reasons can be transmitted, communicated, explained by critics and artists alike to any audience.

In other words, what the modernist offers a confused and tradition-bound audience filled with fear and superstition is a way to rationalize everything in the world. All natural phenomena are explicable in principle (even if details are still wanting), and all power relations can be justified (in terms of precedent or merit). That is to say, one can find the reasons why something is the case in every arena under study. This posture legitimates two interrelated situations: on the one hand, there are criteria of classification and demarcation, and on the other hand, there are experts that can adjudicate between competing claims for those classifications and demarcations and set the record straight! This posture remains alive as we look back into the past century, with art critics and theorists (Clement Greenberg and Arthur Danto, to name two familiar ones). What they offer in turn is a legitimation of their own pronouncements and judgments about what these artists do and how well they do what they do. This secondary feature of self-legitimation eventually gets picked up as a postmodernist posture, since any self-legitimation is itself suspect and cannot, by definition, make an appeal to any foundation, criteria, or even the traditional power of a divinity. As we shall see later, it's this chronology of aesthetics events (experiences, productions, and judgments) that allows someone like Jean-François Lyotard to claim that the postmodern is in fact a "nascent" condition of the modern. The one set of conditions leads to another, and the one set of productions leads to another, a similar but also different condition.

Even when contemporary avant-garde art (as opposed to the general label *modern art*) is associated with more impressionistic or romantic tendencies in the past two centuries, there are salient variables that can be detected even in the quest for the sublime, since there is a necessary or inevitable rejection of traditional or overly personal aesthetic expressions. We discussed some of the predicaments facing avant-garde artists elsewhere (Sassower & Cicotello 2006). For example, the leading American art critic of the mid-twentieth century, Clement Greenberg, in his landmark essay, "Avant-Garde and Kitsch" of 1939, has his set of criteria according to which to demarcate between authentic and inspiring art that revolutionizes the aesthetic community and "art" that is uninteresting, repetitive, and mass produced. He says:

> The nonrepresentational or "abstract," if it is to have aesthetic validity, cannot be arbitrary and accidental, but must stem from obedience to some worthy constraint or original. This constraint, once the world of common, extraverted experience has been renounced, can

only be found in the very processes or disciplines by which art and literature have already imitated the former. (Greenberg 1961, 6)

Kitsch, he continues, "using for raw material the debased and acade-micized simulacra of genuine culture . . . Kitsch is mechanical and operates by formulas. Kitsch is vicarious experience and faked sen-sation . . . Kitsch is the epitome of all that is spurious in the life of our times" (Ibid., 10). Greenberg is modernist in the sense of setting boundaries between good and evil, beautiful and ugly, authentic and fake, avant-garde art and Kitsch. He has used his set of criteria to make or break the careers of artists, to promote or demote artistic movements and schools, single-handedly conferring the status of art on what fit within his theoretical (and rule-bound) framework. His modernist gesture, though seemingly an aesthetic judgment, ends up being the work of a power-broker intent on legitimating one set of artworks as opposed to another.

Arthur Danto, a contemporary New York art critic and theorist, similarly falls within the more contemporary tendencies of mod-ern aesthetic theorists, despite an appearance of genteel openness to anything new or novel. In "Art after the End of Art," Danto explains his own contribution to the discussion of the Death of Art, itself a declaration of period-setting, of articulating boundary conditions for something that we call art. He claims that his "thesis of the end of art was not in the least an ideological one." Rather, he continues, "my thought was that art came to an end when it achieved a philosophical sense of its own identity, and that meant that an epic quest, beginning some time in the latter part of the nineteenth century, had achieved closure" (Danto 1994, 324). For him, "moving pictures" replaced paintings, and as such a new era dawned on the art world. Danto, too, succumbs to the fashionable modernist zest for periodization. The shocking labels "the death of art" or "the end of art" are meant to be provocative if not ideologi-cal, but in fact denote no such thing. Indeed, they denote the death or end of this or that specific use of this or that specific medium within this or that conceptual boundaries. But this says very little about one's aesthetic experience in general and only helps explain particular (visual or sensual) responses under particular material and ideological conditions.

The very distinction between modern and postmodern aesthetics is itself a concession to modernity. In some respects, the very distinction is blurred or remains confusing, as is the case when "American Modernism" is associated with "Stieglitz, Duchamp, and the New York Avant-Garde" (Balken 2003), while some would regard those very artists as postmodern through and through. So, we should hasten to add, in Lyotard's spirit, that the designation of modern and postmodern is not dependent on any periodization, but rather is meant in the sense that different trends or tendencies can be observed; in fact, they both can coexist simultaneously and be seen picking up each other's neglected pieces (see Lyotard & Thebaud 1985, 16). The postmodern condition, whether understood in Lyotard's sense or anyone else's, is one where tradition is interlaced with the modern tendencies to regularity and structure, reason and rationality. It's a situation wherein one need not choose between opposing or contradictory tendencies, but in which one can embrace them all simultaneously. The acceptance of a multitude of styles and genres, or attitudes and media—from painting to sculptures to jewelry—is not an escape from aesthetic judgment, but rather an appreciation of the impossibility in the postmodern world to reduce all aesthetic expressions and experiences into one or two sets of criteria or boundary conditions.

What is fascinating about the so-called postmodern aesthetics of Lyotard is his reliance on and emergence from the Kantian framework, especially when it comes to the notion of the sublime, that which is the ultimate aesthetic experience that stands at the boundary of one's daily experiences. As he says:

> The sublime such as Kant analyzes it in *Critique of Judgment* offers, in the context of quite another problematic, some traits. . . . It introduces what . . . will be an aesthetics of shock, an anesthetics. . . . It is a shock that . . . defies the power that is nevertheless constitutive of the mind according to Kant. . . . Not only does the imagination, required to present sensibly something that would re-present the Absolute,

fail in its task to but it falls into an "abyss." . . . When the sublime is "there" (where?), the mind is not there. As long as the mind is there, there is no sublime. This is a feeling that is incompatible with time, as is death. . . . There is, however, a sublime feeling. And Kant even qualified it as the combination of pleasure and pain . . . this nucleus of the Kantian thesis . . . is anticipated in so-called modern art. (Lyotard 1990, 31–33)

It's in this sense that Lyotard looks back at Kant, the great Enlightenment German philosopher, as the one who set the stage for departing from the modern to the postmodern, from rational deconstruction and self-reflection to the emotional level where feelings dominate and cannot be deconstructed in the Kantian manner. These additional factors require a Freudian appeal to the subconscious, for example, to deeper levels of denial, repression, and sublimation, or a whole new set of ideas and frameworks. The focus on the sublime, then, becomes the focus on the lines of rationality that are *crossed over* and that permit no return. In Lyotard's words: "What art can do is bear witness not to the sublime, but to this aporia of art and to its pain. It does not say unsayable, but says that it cannot say it" (Ibid., 47). Once again, Kant's skeleton of the sublime—the idea that the sublime is beyond rational deconstruction—is brought out of the closet, for he, too, seems to have been a postmodernist of sorts, talking about that which we cannot talk. Elsewhere Lyotard asks:

How is one to understand the sublime, or, let us say provisionally, the object of a sublime experience, as a "here and now"? . . . Between the seventeenth and eighteenth centuries in Europe this contradictory feeling—pleasure and pain, joy and anxiety, exaltation and depression—was christened or re-christened by the name of the *sublime*. . . . It is in this name that aesthetics asserted its critical rights over art, and that romanticism, in other words, modernity, triumphed. (Lyotard 1991, 89–92)

Modernity dealt with emotional tensions intellectually, following the traditional line up to Spinoza with the conviction that the mind could control the heart, that we can rationalize ourselves out of our

emotional mess and take control over our behavior and our interactions with others. Even the sublime conformed to some level of
rational analysis, at least to the extent that it designated a boundary
position.

Lyotard continues: "With the advent of the aesthetics of the sublime, the stake of art in the nineteenth and twentieth centuries was
to be the witness to the fact that there is indeterminacy" (Ibid., 101).
Indeterminacy became an acceptable concept by the late twentieth
century with Einstein and Heisenberg and the development of
quantum mechanics as a framework that overshadows the classical
Cartesian and Baconian quest for certainty which had become untenable. Incidentally, the notion of indeterminacy in science spilled
over to other fields of research, such as economics, so that when
models of economic equilibrium in the marketplace are discussed,
it's understood that they represent ideal types in Weber's sense. As
such, they are heuristic tools with which to comprehend the overwhelming disequilibria that permeate the economic world.

What makes Lyotard's discussion of the sublime so interesting
isn't only that he evokes Kant everywhere, but that he links it to
areas other than the art world. For example, when explaining the
"collusion between capital and avant-garde," Lyotard argues that
"there is something of the sublime in capitalist economy" (Ibid.,
105). The very idea of wealth accumulation is sublime-like because
it overshadows and defies actual instances in reality, yet one's feelings and experiences of it are definitely real. This is a postmodern
move or practice because Lyotard is intent on illustrating the inter-
disciplinary nature of all research and exploration, and that one set
of examples always remains on par with others, interlaced in unexpected ways and thus inevitably interrelated. This doesn't mean
that the modernists were wrong in setting boundaries and making
distinctions all along, helping to provide rational grounds as foundation for critical discourse ever since Socrates. Rather, their intellectual efforts should be seen as useful attempts to fulfill specific goals,
like political peace or universal aesthetics, and as such, they have no
essential features or characteristics that remain immutable to different analyses within different contexts. Put differently, no standard

or fundamental parameters and criteria can be used across different contexts under the postmodern banner.

Lyotard reminds us that Kant cites the Biblical injunction against making "graven images" of the divine. This, of course, was meant as a reminder to avoid the polytheistic and pagan practices of the ancients who worshipped multiple idols. The Jews (and the Muslims later) took this to heart and suppressed artistic creativity, remaining within the confines of the written word. Roman Catholics (in contrast to their East Orthodox brethren) ignored this commandment and set in motion almost two thousand years of fabulous artworks, the bulk of what we call today the history of Western art, financed by and prominently displayed in churches around the globe. What was forbidden, as far as Kant and Lyotard suggest, was the representation of the Absolute, the Sublime. Lyotard associates this with avant-garde paintings of the twentieth century that "devote themselves to making an allusion to the unpresentable by means of visible presentations" (Lyotard 1984, 78). For him, this is the underlying reason for the shift to abstraction. "What, then, is the postmodern?" he asks. His quick answer is that "it is undoubtedly a part of the modern." More specifically, "A work can become modern only if it is first postmodern. Postmodernism thus understood is not modernism at its end but in the nascent state, and this state is constant" (Ibid., 79). This, then, is in sharp contrast to Danto's sense of the "end of art" or the "death of art," where one period comes to a closure and the next begins. For Lyotard, the one is part of the other, the one allows for the emergence of the other, and the one remains a necessary condition for the other, in a very dialectical manner. While the modern artist struggles with the presentation of the sublime without success, the postmodern artist relishes this process as an illustration of the impossible, the predicament with which one must be content, self-consciously highlighting it, and celebrating the invention of the rules according to which art should be pursued (Ibid., 81).

In order to illustrate how this highly theoretical discussion has some contemporary application, it may be useful to shift it to the commercial arena of art: its production, distribution, and consumption. The refusal of the hegemony of styles or the hierarchy of talents that characterizes postmodernism plays well, among other places, into the diverse commercial realities of the southwest art world (e.g., Indian Market in Santa Fe as well as the numerous galleries in the city center). This sampling defies the simple divide commonly adopted by academies and art institutes in regards to the difference between modernism and postmodernism. It also undermines the putative authority of curators and art critics, museum directors and gallery owners, not to mention collectors and the general public that attends openings and shows. Within the context of the southwest, one encounters the intrusion of artists, such as Georgia O'Keefe, who have juxtaposed their modernist ideals with the local landscape (that is neither modern nor postmodern). What does it mean to have a museum dedicated to her work? What does it mean to argue about the inevitable development of her work within this environment?

Let's survey some of the salient aesthetic components one finds in Santa Fe, the third most important American center of commercial art. First, there are museums, ranging from the Museum of International Folk Art to the Georgia O'Keeffe Museum. Second, there are numerous galleries, along Canyon Road, around the Square, and at the Rail Yard, most of which display "southwestern art," namely, paintings and sculptures of Native Americans, an infinite variety of howling Coyotes, and bright red desert sunsets; and of course, some display abstract works of art by aspiring young avant-gardists or displaced New York artists. Third, there are shops and galleries that display folk art, ranging from Kokopelli and dream-catchers to other small sculptures, baskets, and blankets. Fourth, there is the featured Indian Market, sometimes scheduled in the summer and one that is year-round with peddlers along the Governors' Palace Arcade. Finally, there is Site Santa Fe Contemporary Art Space, the attempt to be hip-nouveau-serious-artsy, drawing on national and international artists with exhibitions dedicated to a theme or specific installation projects in mind. Given this broad spectrum of appearances and examples, one wonders what aesthetic judgment can be made, if any at all, and if one is rendered, how inclusive or exclusive would it be?

Just like New York and Paris, St. Petersburg and Mexico City, we find ourselves with the embarrassment of riches, where no single assessment or single criterion of demarcation or classification can be validated, for any judgment is as good as any other. What makes Santa Fe more interesting than any of these other cultural centers is its size: its constitutive members and components are in such close proximity that they seem to seamlessly interlace. For example, one can view Santa Fe as the refuge of successful New York artists, such as Georgia O'Keeffe, who sought in the wide southwestern horizons the kind of bright and clear light and surface openness that couldn't be found in urban settings. Similarly, one can view Santa Fe as the repository of Native American folk art, where indigenous "authenticity" can be bought for less than $100. One needn't go to the pueblos and walk among the natives, since their products are readily available at any air-conditioned store in town. Moreover, the museums in town are the best tourist attractions for family vacations that have a cultural component in them to supplement sheer commercial delight of shopping malls and open-air markets. Likewise, the galleries in town claim to bring the latest and best of American artists, suggesting in every venue that Santa Fe ranks among the top three art markets in the country in terms of sales. New Yorkers on vacation here end up buying the work of New York artists who show in SoHo or Chelsea, but have no time to go shopping for artworks during their normal working schedule. And finally, Site Santa Fe is literally across the tracks, so it is supposed to be an alternative for all that is wrong with the rest of Santa Fe's art scene: it's cool, it's different, and in many cases it's foreign!

As these brief examples illustrate, there is something postmodern in the aesthetic experience in the southwest, but something that can easily be turned into and fall under the modernist spell. Of course one can classify and demarcate, use one's rational faculties to appreciate and distinguish the authentic from the commercial, the good from the bad. Even when undertaken ironically, such assessment is always at hand; but what brings us closer to the present century is that the authority of a Greenberg or a Danto or a Lyotard is no longer needed; anyone can be an art critic, no matter how poor the critique is done. This aesthetic empowerment doesn't preclude the demand for aesthetic rigor or knowledge, mastery of the history of art and art criticism. Yet, the standards themselves get reevaluated and recast with every new generation, and as such this process opens the door for multiple judgments based on multiple standards. Herein lies the promise or doom of postmodern aesthetics. No wonder modern aesthetics remains appealing.

FABRICATING WAR IMAGES

Even art theorists, such as Ernst Gombrich (1960), who are more concerned with the psychological elements that inform our visual perspectives, define avant-garde art (modern in some historic renditions) in terms of "nonfigurative art" and associate it with twentieth-century art. There are the modernist-formalists, such as Roger Fry (1934—on British art) and Clement Greenberg, already mentioned (1961), whose concern is with the conventions that inform each stage of aesthetic production and appreciation. For them, the very definition of what is considered art is tenable, as well as the value and meaning of that art. All of them are gate-keepers of sorts who can tell us sometimes why this is art and what kind of art it is, since they are the aesthetic rainmakers of the present. In some respects, each art critic has been able to determine the acceptability of pieces of art within the artistic community and with the public at large: criteria have been set, such as representation, form, content, style, medium, context, social message, so as to set apart or bring together various artists and their productions into a "school" or "movement."

While some claim that modernist aesthetics can be clearly *read* according to a set of criteria (however historically informed), there are those who claim that this kind of reading is too rigid, even hegemonic. As mentioned in the previous section, postmodern aesthetics has been offered as an alternative to modern aesthetics, one that opens up to multiple interpretations according to multiple sets of criteria (see Hoesterey's collection of 1991). This openness has been lauded as both liberating and empowering, encouraging theoretical and practical participation from diverse groups whose own voices were historically marginalized. The postmodernist posture begins with a protest, a refusal to admit a single definition for art and likewise, a disruptive attempt to redefine accepted definitions, expand and revise, undermine and break down that which the artistic establishment has claimed to be the case. It almost doesn't matter who says what about art, since whatever is being said is bound to be challenged as a matter of course, so that the definitions of the modern and postmodern are less meaningful than the consequences of actually producing artworks. One example that jumps to the fore is Marcel Duchamp's insertion of a "ready-made" urinal (or in his title, "the Fountain") into a "fine-art" exhibit in 1917. The very attempt to define art once and for all becomes an occasion for defiance and for rethinking that which has been defined. This is not to say that there is no definition of or for art pieces, but rather that whatever is suggested remains open-ended, putative, and conjectural (in the Popperian sense, 1963).

It is in this spirit that any discussion of art and aesthetics remains an invitation and solicitation, a way to get more people involved in the debate over the value of art and the ways in which meanings are injected into it. In short, this is recognition of the temporality of what we create and observe, the artifacts that surround us. Put differently, it is a way to engage the art world and ourselves, reexamining our prejudices and convictions, and expressing our willingness to participate in an adventure. Indeed, the postmodern condition in general and in the art arena in particular has forced us to reconsider our perception of political images that subsume an ideological commitment regardless of a prefigured artistic intent. Whether we admit to it or not, we all subscribe to an ideology, a set of ideas and convictions that guide our life and the choices we make. Let us detail this reconsideration, relying to some extent on a similar conceptual and perceptual structure we discuss elsewhere (Sassower & Cicotello 2006).

The argument here is divided into three steps in regards to war images. First, there is the step that connects data, facts in the field, so to speak, with pictorial images (the visual). Second, there is the presentation of images in the popular media as means of explaining the war to the public (the explanatory). And third, there are the ways in which images are read by the public regardless of what they were meant to convey (the perceptual). Let us elaborate briefly on the three steps or stages, and then explain why the postmodern option of reading images, though appealing in various ways, may turn out to be more problematic than the modern one.

Already in the 1920s Otto Neurath explained how powerful, useful, and socially progressive it was to use images rather than difficult and cumbersome arguments (1925, International System of Typographic Picture Education). Though there are problems of representation regardless of the medium, whether words are used to represent reality (in Wittgenstein's early, 1922, and late, 1958, senses) or models of the marketplace are used to represent the economy, images have always been welcomed by politicians (campaign and propaganda posters). Through images, politicians hope to convey a message, an idea, or a set of ideologically refined principles. An image of a wholesome family, whether drawn by the American Norman Rockwell or propagated by the Nazis, immediately conveys a certain set of commitments: to one's family, to one's ancestry, to one's religious beliefs, all the way to heterosexual procreation and hopes for harmony and happiness. Here we unsuspectingly gaze at a whole set of ideals that eventually get internalized and that might be questioned and undermined in a more diverse and multi-cultural context, where heterosexuality and homogeneity, for example, are not taken for granted as the only standards according to which to establish and assess human relations. So, the first stage of the argument deals with the relationship between images and the events or facts they are supposed to represent. How does one represent the reality of wars? Is this about battle scenes or about personal devastation? Can one recreate the reality of pain, suffering, and heroism? Can an arrested image ever convey the fluidity of events and their context?

The second step of the argument deals with the specific context within which images are distributed and consumed, the particular media in which they are presented. For example, should a war image be presented only in the internal documents of government agencies or be leaked to the press? Is it more prestigious or credible for an image to appear in a newspaper rather than on the Internet? Obviously it matters which newspaper is used, for there are some, like the National Inquirer in the USA, that are notorious for fabricating or manipulating images to such an extent that they are no longer seen as being "real" or "credible." But once the extremes of the media are excluded, such as hate-group websites and the like, is there a hierarchy of credibility? Is there a way for all of us to know and to agree on a set of criteria from which to judge which print-media is more or less credible than another? This is reminiscent of the debates over the authenticity of photographs and documentaries, black-and-white images that seem more detached and real than those characterized by color differentiation.

Some Americans are prone to believe that anything the government says is true and that whatever appears on television is "real," no matter what the circumstances. One can view the popularity of "reality shows" as an indicator of the perception that if it is shown on television, then it must be real and true. Similarly, the Paparazzi can always find a willing newspaper that will pay top dollar to see what real celebrities look like up close and what they are doing in their private lives! Of course the complexity of these assertions is compounded by the fact that some networks and media channels are public, in the sense of receiving government grants and having to abide by some government regulations, and others are not. Should one give the same (public interest) status to a news outlet that increases revenues through advertising and that invests in sensationalist broadcasting in order to increase viewership/readership to justify higher advertising rates?

It is within this context of public and private reporting that we confront the problem of how and where to present war images, that is, how gruesome or benign the images should be, whether to invoke patriotism and support for the troops or be subject to objections for failing to do so. If the first step of the argument is about the content of the image and its relation to what it is supposed to represent, then the second step of the argument is about the format and context of representation in general, whether of war images or the economy, whether one chooses newsprint, television, or the Internet.

The third step of the argument is what was described elsewhere (Sassower and Cicotello 2006) as the predicament of having images read differently from the intent of the creator or sponsor. There we examined a variety of public displays, such as monuments and posters, from the Soviet Union, Italy, Germany, Mexico, and the United States in the period between the two World Wars. We discovered to our amazement and amusement that though diametrically opposed ideologues thought they were putting forth a powerful message through posters, meant to invoke patriotism and support for all their respective regimes, they tended to use similar, and at times identical, images. For example, one can find the same "hand with a hammer" in posters from the era between the two world wars from the Soviet Union, the United States, fascist Italy, Nazi Germany, and Mexico. Our limited survey could have been extended to amplify the universal nature of this image. For example, one can find a Canadian poster, titled "It's Our War" from WWII that copied a cropped image of the hand and hammer from the Italian fascist poster of 1934 we identified in our own book (see Ibid., xi and 61). This means that once an image is put out in public, the public can read it however it wants, interpret it in a fashion that may not be what was originally intended.

There is, then, no linear or causal connection between an idea, its image, and its reading by someone else. Instead, a fascist or democratic reading can be gained from the same image: courage and heroism, diligence and commitment, national pride and camaraderie, family value and wholesome friendship. Who does not want them? Who would not endorse them? So, the third step of the argument is about the inherent ambiguity of images and the ways in which they lend themselves to multiple interpretations, none of which is the "right" one (except in the minds of the authorities who are responsible for their production).

In what follows, we would like to suggest that however appealing postmodern aesthetics may seem, there is a high political and moral price to be paid when eschewing modernist aesthetics with its interpretive clarity. We all welcome the openness offered by the postmodern move as a way to read images however we choose, without the legitimating authority of politicians, in the case of wars, who justify military involvement or specific strategies to be used. It is perhaps this openness that ensures a critical dimension, a way to keep politicians honest and accountable for their decisions, suggesting that their decisions may end up in retrospect more problematic than they appeared at first. Our involvement in assessing images, of course, is already too late and inevitably compromised, since we have no access to the data that prompt the use of these or other images. Politicians and military leaders make decisions based on confidential information and then portray their decisions pictorially for public consumption. Here and there, photojournalists intervene, sometime on behalf of the authorities, sometimes in a subversive way so as to expose the weakness of decisions and their folly. As the Roman Catholic tradition of moral philosophy has taught us, *just war* principles can sanction wars but also can illustrate the conditions under which one should not wage a war. Historically, wars have been waged for economic reasons, both domestic and colonial, to boost faltering political careers, and for sheer ignorance or arrogance. It is difficult at times to distinguish among these reasons, as they tend to merge and be self-serving along the way (especially when there are unintended consequences to the way in which ideas and images are eventually consumed).

THE PREDICAMENT OF FRAMING WAR IMAGES

The focus of the examples chosen in chapter 2 (four images of eight different wars or conflicts), is from a variety of combat-arenas. These images can be crudely divided into those that can be read through the modernist prism, namely, as if they can be read in a straightforward manner: here are the facts, the reality that is captured by a camera with little ambiguity or confusion. Surely, one can add an interpretive layer to any reading, but let us refrain from this additional step at first and see what we come up with. Then there are those images that can be read through the postmodern prism, namely, as if there is no single reading that captures the meaning or the reality or the facts of the matter: one can agree on reading some elements in the image across cultural lines, but there is much room for interpretation, and for emphasis on which elements to highlight or ignore.

The contention here is that it is precisely with war images (as represented in the media) that we come to the realization that interpretive manipulation is not merely a theoretical *game* (in Lyotard's sense, 1984) but an enormously problematic and dangerous undertaking, akin to the worst fascist propaganda mechanisms of the past century. If all we know of the current wars in Iraq and Afghanistan, for example, is what is presented to us through official American channels (with strict military censorship), it may seem that it is a just war, a war for democracy, and a winnable war with little harm and suffering. Leni Riefenstahl, who notoriously chronicled in her film, *Triumph of the Will*, Hitler's rise to power and his immense popular appeal, would feel right at home within this propagandist context, when national pride and patriotic zeal overshadowed any and all critical disturbances. Should we then revert back to modernist aesthetics in its classical guise, so as to expose manipulation and misleading images? Or should we provide intellectual frameworks that would alert audiences to the context within which images should be read?

It may be helpful to conclude here with a brief description of *just war theory* so as to explain some of the underlying issues that may be simmering below the political and the journalistic surface. Perhaps in doing so, we can more fully appreciate our own cognitive confusion and psychological discomfort when confronting war images. We will be following both Alexander Moseley (2005) to illustrate the main arguments and principles associated with the justification for waging wars, and Robert Kolb (1997) to appreciate some of the misconceptions associated with the term. For example, though Latin is used to distinguish between the causes and the conduct of war (*jus ad bellum* and *jus in bello*), these expressions were only coined at the time of the League of Nations and were rarely used in doctrine or practice until after the Second World War in the late 1940s. What all nations that experienced the war worried about was providing a legal framework within which the problems of "might makes right" could be dealt with rationally, consistently, and fairly. The classical concerns of fighting with dignity for an honorable cause have been historically transformed into a more concrete framework that acquired an international audience and legitimacy.

First, there is a theoretical framework that follows five major principles, all of which should hold in order to wage a just war. These are: having just cause, being declared by a proper authority, possessing right intention, having a reasonable chance of success, and the end being proportional to the means used. Possessing a *just cause* is the first and arguably the most important condition of *jus ad bellum*. Most theorists hold that initiating acts of aggression is unjust and gives a group a just cause to defend itself. But, as the *Encyclopedia Britannica* reminds us, unless "aggression" is defined, this proscription is rather open-ended. For example, just cause resulting from an act of aggression can ostensibly be a response to a physical injury (e.g., a violation of territory), an insult (an aggression against national honor), a trade embargo (an aggression against economic activity), or even a neighbor's prosperity (a violation of social justice). The main argument regarding the initiation of war is self-defense. The Christian interpretation of "thou shall not kill" from the Ten Commandments is stricter than the Jewish one which eventually finds its way into legal systems as degrees of culpability. Of course, the notion of "self-defense" can itself be stretched, as the United States has repeatedly done, so as to justify pre-emptive strikes, as in the war in Iraq. The threat, it was suggested by the Bush administration (2001–2008), was so grave with weapons of mass destruction that it was a matter of "when" and not "if" Saddam Hussein would be attacking the Western world.

The second condition that must be met in order to conduct just war has to do with the authority of the party declaring war. Should it be a government? What kind of a government qualifies? Must it be democratically elected? As the *Encyclopedia* suggests, some governments are more appropriately recognized as the ones with unchallenged authority. The Vichy puppet regime, set up in 1940 by the invading Germans, deserved no public support from French citizens who did not elect it. Here we come to questions of sovereignty as discussed historically by a range of political philosophers who insisted, ever since the trial of Socrates, that there must exist an underlying contract among all participants so that the government is merely a representative of the General Will (to use Rousseau's terminology). The people remain the sovereign power and have the ultimate authority in all state matters, domestic and international alike. The only condition for conferring any authority on the government is that when acting it indeed represents the will of the people and secondly, that when it does not, it can be removed without violence (through recall, impeachment, election, or referenda).

The third condition for waging a just war is that there should be a right or appropriate intention. The general thrust of the concept being that a nation waging a just war should be doing so for the cause of justice and not for reasons of self-interest or aggrandizement. Of course, moral theorists have some problems with this being a sufficient (though would allow for it to remain a necessary) condition for just war. What happens if the right intention leads to many unfortunate and unintended consequences? For example, is it possible to draw a clear line between right intention and self-interest, especially when debating the vague notion of national self-interest in the preservation of equal rights or freedom around the globe? Does the fact that according to foreign observers certain parts of a population seem to lack basic human freedoms justify an invasion for democratic liberation, as was argued in the case of the Iraq War?

The fourth condition or another necessary condition for waging a just war is that of reasonable success. Perhaps one way of thinking about this condition is in terms of a quixotic fight against evil monsters regardless of the outcome. Perhaps this sounds reasonable insofar as there are no costs or damages suffered in the process (except for a wounded ego or two). Yet, in cases of domestic oppression by a police state, does it matter if one were to stand up to a bullying aggressor, knowing full-well that no benefits could emerge (except for gaining some self-esteem or national pride)? Should a sovereign state aid foreign people or declare war on moral grounds even if there is no conceivable chance of success? One could think of this condition, then, primarily as a deterrent to frivolous declaration of war when there is no chance to defeat another army, so that the costs borne by the nation would not be disproportionate to what gains may be imagined. Many critics of the war in Iraq claim it has always been an un-winnable war, because a military offensive against civilian insurgents is bound to fail, as it did in the Vietnam War. Complete annihilation has always been the strategy of choice for those hoping for complete surrender.

The final guide or condition of a just war is that the desired end should be proportional to the means used. This principle overlaps into the moral guidelines of how a war should be fought, namely the principles of *Jus in Bello*. This means-ends matrix is designed to ensure that minimal provocations do not license another nation to overwhelm and destroy the instigator. This principle, used routinely in courts of law, ensures that the punishment fits the crime, so to speak. After the Japanese attack on Pearl Harbor during World War II, the United States felt justified in dropping atomic bombs on Hiroshima and Nagasaki in Japan, killing more than one hundred thousand civilians. Is the killing of more than fifty thousand Iraqi citizens (as reported in the UK) since the beginning of the second Iraq War the right moral "proportion" of civilian destruction?

Historically, questions related to just war theory had to justify or provide the conditions that ought to be met in order to declare war on another nation (and that can be retrospectively deemed just) as well as the guiding principles according to which a war should be conducted. Though Biblical references are inconsistent in permitting looting and even rape and enslavement, there is a sense already in that text regarding the just conduct of wars sanctioned by God. Has one fought honorably? Has one treated prisoners of war fairly, at least in the Kantian sense of treating them the way one would like to be treated? These questions were resolved much later (in the Geneva Convention of 1949), so that international standards could be appealed to. Moreover, as the two world wars of the twentieth century taught us, "crimes against humanity" is an actionable designation that can land a leader or a soldier in the International Court in The Hague. In general, these principles, according to Moseley, can be divided into three.

The first moral principle relates to the appropriate targets of war, so that innocent bystanders or civilians are excluded. Obviously, once in the throws of battle, this kind of discrimination becomes difficult, especially, as the United States has often done, when the targets are not directly seen since air-strikes drop bombs from thousands of feet above ground. No matter how "smart" the bombs are, they may land on the wrong targets either because of faulty intelligence or operational errors. The second principle relates to how much force is appropriate to use in war (as already discussed). The third principle relates to responsibility, who should be held accountable for killing or for destroying the enemy? Is it the soldier who pulls the trigger of a machine gun, the pilot who releases a bomb above a city, or the generals sitting at headquarters miles away but ordering specific actions? One can take it a step further and ask if it is the politicians, who voted to launch the war, that are ultimately responsible for atrocities committed in the field. Elsewhere (Sassower 1997), it has been suggested that scientists and engineers should be held responsible for the projects they have worked on and for developing theories and devices that have the potential to be used against humans.

But here, too, there are moral problems that cannot be easily dismissed or glossed over. Each term is inherently problematic and raises new questions. What counts as a "threat" by someone? Must it be direct or is indirect sufficient? Who count as "noncombatants"? Without support of munitions and gas and food, no battle could be waged, so even civilian mobilization for a war effort can be seen as direct engagement in the war effort. Are acts of "aggression" necessarily limited to force or occupation or are economic and financial terms sufficient? Hence raising tariffs or nationalizing private industries could be deemed just cause for military action. Michael Walzer (1977), for example, argues that the concept of "war" was transformed once nuclear bombs were introduced into the arsenal of nation-states (and more recently to rogue regimes and fringe militant organizations as well). The potential for having such weapons, as seen today in the case of Iran and North Korea, has brought about international intervention (sanctions, threats, talks, and agreements). While ownership of nuclear weaponry can give cause for pre-emptive strike, the international community is loath to give this license automatically.

It is with *just war theory* in mind, that one should examine images of war and terrorism. If the moral issues are related both to the causes and the proper conduct of war, and if these issues come to light in specific cases, then one photo or image of an event or situation, a battle or a victory, seems to encapsulate everything that is right or wrong about a war. We are prone to summarize hundreds of arguments and particular instances of a protracted war in an aesthetic visual moment, glancing at a pictorial representation as if it says it all. But this temptation of simplification must also alert us to the possibility that political or military leaders can censor or promote a specific image in order to justify a war or condemn the enemy, however they construe them. The potential for image manipulation is so great nowadays—even greater than before because of the introduction of digital technology—that we believe it to be our responsibility to warn *readers* of war images of this potential. In the postmodern context, where advanced technological devices are cheap and accessible enough to proliferate outside established media networks (that are regulated), one needs to be alert. This is not to say that some so-called modernist framework (with rigid criteria and set pre-judgments) will protect us from simple-minded temptations of clear-cut assessments. Rather, this is to say that as tempting as the ongoing advent of image technology may be, it is dangerous as well.

Perhaps the critical dimension of image producers, photojournalists, documentary movie directors, and other artists can surface when we juxtapose a variety of images and contrast them with one another so as to distill a more nuanced version of a war, with all of its heroic and patriotic acts as well as its suffering and devastation.

There are no guarantees, of course, but only promissory notes about the need to educate ourselves to be more critical in our aesthetic engagement with war images. This recommendation, as we shall examine in more detail in the next chapter, is pragmatic as well: if one is to evaluate foreign policies, one needs to be able to ask the right questions, and be skeptical if and when one is presented with a simple, singular image which pretends to substitute a thousand words. The theoretical framing of modernists and postmodernist aesthetics, as we have seen, remain painfully inadequate for the task. What may salvage the best of their characterization and insights is a thoroughly critical engagement that skeptically views any claim for moral certainty and clear vision.

2

WAR IMAGES

In this chapter there is a selection of images from eight wars from the 1800s to the present. The wars they represent are: the Napoleonic Wars: 1792–1815, the American Civil War: 1861–1865, World War I: 1914–1918, World War II: 1939–1945, the War in Afghanistan: 2001–, the two Iraq Wars: 1990–1991; 2003–, and the Palestinian-Israeli Conflict: 1948– .

The sets of four images per war are displayed without commentary or titles, but are followed by representative analyses and a historical annotation. The intent is to allow readers to come up with their own interpretations and supplement the given analyses with their own.

Photo 1. Napoleonic Wars: 1792–1815.
Source: Awesome Art

Photo 4. Napoleonic Wars: 1792–1815. *Source:* AICT

Photo 2. Napoleonic Wars: 1792–1815.
Source: Awesome Art

Photo 3. Napoleonic Wars: 1792–1815. *Source:* AICT

Photo 5. American Civil War: 1861–1865. *Source:* National Archives

Photo 8. American Civil War: 1861–1865. *Source:* National Archives

Photo 6. American Civil War: 1861–1865. *Source:* National Archives

Photo 7. American Civil War: 1861–1865. *Source:* National Archives

Photo 9.   World War I: 1914–1918. *Source:* GWPDA

Photo 12.   World War I: 1914–1918. *Source:* Scottish National Galleries

**Photo 10.   World War I:
1914–1918.** *Source:* GWPDA

**Photo 11.   World
War I: 1914–1918.**
Source: National Archives

Photo 13.   World War II: 1939–1945. *Source:* National Archives

Photo 16.   World War II: 1939–1945. *Source:* USHMM

Photo 14.   World War II: 1939–1945. *Source:* National Archives

Photo 15.   World War II: 1939–1945. *Source:* US Naval Archives

Photo 17.   Vietnam War: 1961–1975.
Source: Hawaii Army Museum

Photo 20.   Vietnam War: 1961–1975. *Source:* NPS

Photo 18. Vietnam War: 1961–1975. *Source:* AP Photo/Adams

Photo 19. Vietnam War: 1961–1975.
Source: Hawaii Army Museum

Photo 21.   The War in Afghanistan: 2001– . *Source:* DHD Gallery/Anonymous

Photo 24.   The War in Afghanistan: 2001– . *Source:* AP Photo/Butler

Photo 22.   The War in Afghanistan: 2001– . *Source:* AP Photo/Thorne

Photo 23.   The War in Afghanistan: 2001– . *Source:* AP Photo/Khan

Photo 25. Two Iraq Wars: 1990–1991; 2003– . *Source:* AP Photo/Mollard

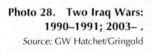

**Photo 28. Two Iraq Wars:
1990–1991; 2003– .**
Source: GW Hatchet/Gringold

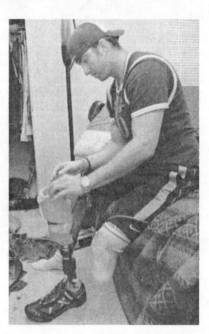

Photo 26. Two Iraq Wars: 1990–1991; 2003– . *Source:* AP Photo/Delay

Photo 27. Two Iraq Wars: 1990–1991; 2003– . *Source:* USAF

Photo 29.   Palestinian-Israeli Conflict: 1948– . *Source:* AP Photo/Hussein

Photo 32.   Palestinian-Israeli Conflict: 1948– . *Source:* Brian Carroll

Photo 30. Palestinian-Israeli Conflict: 1948– . *Source:* AP Photo/HO

Photo 31. Palestinian-Israeli Conflict: 1948– . *Source:* AP Photo/Kami

ANALYSIS OF IMAGES

Before we begin our analysis, we'd like to qualify and explain our choices of images. First, though we have titles for the wars and conflicts we describe, we appreciate how misleading some of them may be. For example, the Iraq War is as much about the nuclear threat of the extremist Islamic regime of Iran as about Iraq proper. Likewise, the Afghanistan War is also about our worries about Pakistan and its nuclear arsenal and its conflict with India and its nuclear arsenal. In short, the labels we use, just as the images we have chosen, are limited in scope and betray a much more complex web of issues and concerns. Perhaps it is exactly this complexity that is being overshadowed when one image or one term is chosen to describe age-old conflicts.

Second, it should be noted that our selection here is problematic as well: why choose these wars and conflicts and not others? When providing a historical survey, it is impossible to do justice to the entire historical record. So, it might be more appropriate to ask: what criteria were used to make the selection? In our case, we tried to complement the American war experience with European ones because we were party to some of them. We also wanted to show the differences in the media that were used to portray wars: charcoal drawings, oil paintings, photographs, and posters. Finally, we chose purposefully some images that are more *canonical* in the American image lexicon so as to analyze the familiar and show its complexities. *Iconic images* seem to tell a story directly and simply; we wish to critically reassess this view.

Third, there are many wars and conflicts that are not documented well or that are not documented at all. This means that the power of the media and journalists working for media outlets is even more pronounced: in their choices they decide what will make it into history books and what will be left out. The ulterior motives of media sources regarding profits and prestige rather than report *objectively* what is happening around the world contribute to what gets reported. At times the issue is fear-mongering so that viewers stay glued to their television sets and more commercials can be broadcasted; at other times, there are political leaders who stake their careers on a particular foreign policy—including waging a war—and pay through campaign funds for media coverage; and still at other times the question may simply be: what images sell newspapers at the newsstand? Few journalists have the freedom to report on what they think is relevant and important, pursuing, as we suggested earlier, *detached engagement*. At the same time, we must distinguish between *professional* journalism and *amateur* reporting, between those who *observe* and those who *participate*, and between those using advanced technologies and those using crude means of transmission. These differences have the power of influencing in varying degrees public perception.

Fourth, our choices can be contested as well as the criteria by which they were made. The simplification that is being displayed here—the few images of a few wars and conflicts—offers an opportunity to reexamine the justification and legitimation of these conflicts, rather than close the discussion. Our own analyses are only samples of what any reader of these images could come up with, depending on their background knowledge and personal experiences.

Napoleonic Wars (1792–1815)

Looking at the four images together will provide a different, more comprehensive view of the Napoleonic Wars than looking at each image in isolation or without reference to any additional images. But if we were to look at the images in isolation, one at a time, this is what we might be *reading*. On the top left we see the heroic leader, thrusting forward with his red cape, pointing his finger upward, to the future of his conquests, to the bright destiny that is his, with a contemplative face burdened with history's fate and its progress. The white horse is emblematic of power and goodness (white always denotes the power of good against evil, the latter being usually denoted by black). The size and the deep color of the cape symbolizes the depth of passion and commitment to his cause of enlightening the entire European continent. Napoleon's victory is ours as well!

The second image on the top right still keeps Napoleon at the center, compositionally speaking. But now he is off his horse, at eye level with his comrades in arms. The boot is off his right leg, since he is injured. The mighty hero and liberator, God's messenger on earth is now revealing his mortality, his wound. The price of victory may be injury and suffering. Despite his own resolution and fearless convictions, the smoke in the background depicts the kind of devastation that comes about in any war: where there are victors, there are vanquished as well. Military might is in the foreground, while civilian casualties are incidents in the background.

The lower right image is of a firing squad in Spain. The Napoleonic troops were not welcomed wherever they went, but were fought by local armies and resistance fighters. Since Napoleon's army had the upper hand militarily, it executed all those who resisted its forward march. The imposition of the Napoleonic Code—the most comprehensive and advanced legal system devised at the time to bring a coherent foundation for European nation-states—was an amazing civic accomplishment on one hand, but a cruel undertaking with many civilian casualties on the other.

The lower left image takes the narrative one step further insofar as it depicts the kind of cruelty and torture imposed on the locals who resisted Napoleon's rule of their native lands. The dismembering of one's body parts so as to put them on stakes in city centers and squares was a common practice to distill fear and intimidation, and undermine the spirit of any local resistance.

Any one of these images alone tells an interesting and historically rich narrative of parts of the Napoleonic Wars. Our brief description of these images scratches the surface and is highly superficial. More of the historical and military data ought to complement such a reading. More stories can be told in each case, and each one of them would represent a different perspective even of the single image under review. For example, we are reminded that Napoleon did not cross the Alps on a white horse but on a mule. So, why paint the white horse? Likewise, *Code Napoleon* was welcomed in Spain as well as in many other countries whose political organization was flawed. So, why foreground resistance and the specter of unfair and cruel torture? What imbedded critique and nationalistic pride are revealed with this visual choice by Goya?

As we mentioned in chapter 1, there could be a *modern* or *post-modern* reading of the images, whether in isolation or together. Either choice, though, would still leave open the question of a possible *universal* language of art, one to which all appeals for objective understanding can be made. This would be helpful, then, for those viewers who'd like to make a moral judgment about the Napoleonic Wars (one or many?): they were justified! They brought progress to Europe! Despite the price of some suffering, the overall benefits outweigh the costs. Finally, one could argue that our Western democratic societies wouldn't be as advanced as they are today without these wars. Some critics would disagree and offer an alternative interpretation: the results of wars are heralded as painless victories by the conquerors, and of course from their perspective (Napoleon's disciples) the wars were justified on a variety of levels, political, economic, social, legal, and moral. But what happened to the vanquished? What voice do they have in reassessing the official judgment of the victors? Their heroes have been vilified as traitors and traditionalists, as backward hacks who couldn't see the values of progress and the future of abundance and freedom.

With this in mind, we begin to appreciate the difficulties of straight-forward assessments of wars, ancient and contemporary. If there were a promise that an image would capture the imagination of the public and ease the anxieties of war-ridden societies, this cursory examination of only *four* representations illustrates how illusory this promise had been. Imagine how more complex the narrative becomes when one hundred pictures and drawings are presented? As we suggest throughout this book, the only cure for this malady is a *critical engagement* that may provide the conditions for pragmatic decision-making.

United States of America Civil War (1861–1865)

The American Civil War brings out a variety of connotations to contemporary audiences, from the great cultural divide that some say still exists between the North and the South, to slave emancipation and the great march forward towards civil rights and race equality, all the way to the patriotic appreciation of diversity among unity (the relationship between the states and the federal government). It would be a folly to try and summarize these views and their attendant ideological commitments. Suffice to say that it was the most devastating war fought on American soil, one that exacted, according to Drew Gilpin Faust (2008), close to a million casualties, both soldiers and civilians, not to mention the destruction and burning of several cities and innumerable farms and plantations. But the war had to be "promoted" by generals and politicians on both sides in order to recruit soldiers and provide funding.

As we look at the first upper left picture, we see a charcoal drawing that is almost surreal, and quite impressionist in style. There is a quickly sketched group of people who might be holding guns; their aim is not at a defined enemy, but could be at hunting targets far away. They are in the woods, and for all we know they are simply hunters not in any military formation or uniform. The sketch is open to anyone's interpretation.

By contrast, the upper right photograph is a clear view of soldiers' corpses left at the end of a battle. The battle is not as significant as the casualty count and getting the bodies buried. The corpses lie scattered across the ground, as if the battle itself had no order and made no sense. Photographs like this one were controversial at the time; some were not printed in newspapers for fear of public outcry and outrage; some were directly censored by military leaders; while some made it into public view. The fact that this is a photograph rather than a drawing made it appear more *real*. To this day, the *reality of images* has been debated in art circles since photography came into popular use in the 1840s.

If *reality* is the focus of the discussion about re-*presenting* events, such as wars, then we should take a close look at the photograph on the lower right side. The photograph depicts a sharpshooter's den which allowed a soldier to hide behind a stone-barrier wall and be an effective sniper hidden from the enemy's view. The gun is leaned against the rock next to the fallen body of the sniper. We may immediately jump to the conclusion that the unfortunate soldier was killed by enemy fire. However, this image was *staged*! Although there were plenty of casualties throughout the war, perhaps this deliberate fabrication tried to distill sympathy from the viewer in regards to the unfortunate or rightly deserved fate that befell this particular soldier.

Contemporary audiences would be hard pressed to appreciate the menacing image of stacked cannonballs, since they are more prone to fear a stack of nuclear bombs piled high at a Russian or North Korean site. On the lower left side we find an image of a Civil War warehouse showing stocked ammunition for the next round of battles. One must appreciate that era's cannons and their effectiveness against particular battle formations. The death toll would be compounded as waves of soldiers walked straight ahead to confront their adversaries face-to-face. One cannonball could break the formation and kill a dozen or so soldiers in a moment, blunt attacks, intimidate with its sound, and cause chaos and death. We can imagine these stocked cannonballs as an abstract installation found in an outdoor sculpture-park. The beauty of the symmetry, the shading of the sunlight, the roundness and the volume of the individual spheres, all add up to what the contemporary art world would find aesthetically appealing.

All of these images create common threads: the suffering of soldiers and their loved ones awaiting their return from the battlefield, the guns used for protection may become the guns that will kill them; the solitary death of the sniper is compounded when placed next to a field of corpses; the destruction caused by cannonballs fired into a group of soldiers becomes evident once the war begins. There is nothing heroic in these images, nothing Napoleonic in grandeur about their representation. Where are the emancipated slaves? Where and how is freedom depicted in these images? What moral justification can be secured from these deaths? Isn't death anything more than death itself? Does it ever transcend its own finality and perhaps futility?

World War I (1914–1918)

If you compare the two images on the top, you realize that both depict trench warfare. During World War I, the strategy on both sides
was to dig long lines of opposing trenches in order to make small
forays into enemy territory, and conquer small swatches of land.
The war was long, it lasted five years, and it involved countries from
around the globe, even though it was fought mainly on European
soil (just as the United States entered the war in 1917, so, for example, did Cuba and Bolivia in the same year). It was truly a "world
war" in this sense of participation. Soldiers spent days and weeks in
the same trench, getting to know not only their fellow-soldiers, but
also their enemies. Legends have it that they would stop artillery
and gun shots on holidays, and even exchange food and wine to celebrate Christmas. So, what distinguishes these two images? Does it
make a difference that on the left the photograph is a square black-
and-white print while on the right it is oval (and sepia toned in the
original)? Does the right one seem more romantic or ambivalent?
Or does the similar subject-matter overshadow whatever visual cues
are being used as props? On the right we see flamethrowers using a
new technical device along with the use of gas to force soldiers out
of their trenches so as to be exposed to enemy fire (new machine
guns were also introduced at the time with the capacity of firing
hundreds of bullets per minute). On the left one can imagine brave
soldiers advancing towards the trenches of their enemy, being
prompted to sacrifice their lives in order to become victorious.

The bottom right poster that declares: "I Want You for U.S.
Army" has become an iconic image of both Uncle Sam—an elderly
and elegant white man pointing his finger at the observer, clad in
a red-white-and-blue outfit as a reminder of the American tri-color
flag—and of our sense of patriotism—where personal sacrifice for
the homeland brings the benefits of democracy and freedom to
the collective American people. Individual voluntarism ends up
appreciated as a collective *good*, so that the country as a whole can
prevail. Incidentally, we have also found a British poster of 1914
with the red caption: "Britons! Your Country Needs You!" on top of

an image of the British isles, from the Parliamentary Recruitment Committee, London 1914. Unlike Switzerland or Israel which impose mandatory conscription, the United States has been reluctant to impose such a policy. The Vietnam War was an exception which brought about waves of conscientious objectors and draft-dodgers. A poster like this reminds us that what makes our nation great are the personal sacrifices that individuals make for their families and their country. What is also significant in this image is that it is a poster, a fairly new medium at the time displayed in public spaces. Just as photography was debated in regards to its representation of reality, so were posters, appearing on billboards, debated in regards to their aesthetics as potentially public nuisance—should they be regulated like the legitimate regulation of urban sanitary conditions? (Bogard 1995). Incidentally, this poster has been continuously used, in numerous versions, since WWI, and has remained *timeless* in its effective appeal.

The last image of this war is the most abstract of the four, and as such could be more widely interpreted. What are these flying machines? Are they a menace or peaceful gliders? What is their scale—are they toys or real airplanes? The famous artist who painted this, Rene Magritte, wanted to evoke the most memorable aspects of the war some twenty years after its conclusion. Just as trench warfare was a strategy employed by both sides, airplanes were also introduced in this war as a new, and in some cases decisive, technological innovation which increased effectiveness for spying missions and offered bombing capabilities. The wonders of flying, as the ancient fantasy of Icarus who used wax to glue feathers to make wings fastened to his body knew all too well, turn out to be devastating. In his case, he came too close to the sun, the wax melted, and he crashed and perished. The specter of overcoming gravity, of reaching up to the sun and moon, demands its toll. There are always unintended consequences associated with the execution of dreams and promises, at times resulting in death. The introduction of airplanes in WWI was likewise a promise that ended in more rather than less devastation, a shift from one technology of destruction to another.

Overall, World War I fails to capture our cultural imagination, like the Napoleonic Wars, nor does it have a specific set of benefits, such as the emancipation of slaves associated with the U.S. Civil War. Rather, it is primarily remembered for its death toll, its length, and by some as a futile waste of resources. Its inconclusiveness and lack of political resolution contributed, according to some, to the onset of World War II. Some have even claimed that World War II was the last great battle of World War I. Perhaps there are no images better fit to represent the war than the ones chosen here: battle scenes, patriotic appeals, and documented details of warfare strategies and tactics with hints of more to come. From one perspective it can be claimed that there is nothing glorified or heroic about this war, nothing to celebrate or honor. There are only painful memories and rows of crosses in cemeteries full of war casualties. From other perspectives, national pride and heroic acts of sacrifice can be enumerated as well as other claims about geopolitical strategies.

World War II (1939–1945)

Images of World War II are more recent in our memory: we may know parents or grandparents who fought in the "War of the Greatest Generation." We may see on the evening news political leaders commemorating D-Day or laying wreaths at national monuments. In many ways, this war more closely represents the symbol of American prowess and justice, fighting for freedom across the globe. The famous photograph depicting the American flag being raised on Iwo Jima has captured the public imagination and has become a symbol of heroism and victory, camaraderie in the face of danger, and the sacrifices we are willing to make on behalf of our country. But even that image, as we have learned by now, was staged, like the staging of the Civil War sniper previously discussed. In retrospect, American *exceptionalism*, as opposed to its previous *isolationism* (called by some xenophobia), has proven to be our newly discovered national pride. Americans were hailed as liberators and humanitarians: the Marshall Plan was deployed in Europe to reconstruct its economy, and funding to rebuild our nemesis Japan, who would go on to become a world leader within a generation, was granted. Numerous images can portray this victorious and monumental effort undertaken by American troops abroad and American civilians at home: from photographs of U.S. tanks enthusiastically welcomed on the streets of Paris to Rosie the Riveter showing that *even* women contributed to the war effort. So, which image would you choose, and why?

Unlike the lack of *closure* of World War I, which inevitably led to World War II, there seems to be some definite conclusions to this war. The top right image reminds us all how wars should not be fought: dropping atomic bombs shifted the strategies of war from conventional methods to unfathomable annihilation that endangered the entire globe. The mushroom cloud depicted in this photograph remains a horrifying reminder that this should never happen again. The Cold War, which lasted through the 1950s and 1960s, affirmed this reminder: the United States and its allies along with the Soviet Union and its satellite states accumulated nuclear bombs. Neither side would pull the trigger, nor, more accurately, push the button. No one was suicidal enough to risk complete destruction, and as such, they maintained a stand-off. The image of the mushroom cloud was a constant reminder of what would happen under conditions of nuclear warfare.

The left image of the war's consequences is more personal and more pleasant: a kiss. The universal appeal of this moment, a moment of national celebration translated into a personal moment, is what the war is all about. A war is fought by individual soldiers and not by collective armies, and as such the individual within the group must be recognized. Fighting soldiers dream of coming home more than killing an enemy: the sweet revenge is coming home alive, and being able to consummate one's hopes and dreams with a kiss, a symbol of love and connection, and of our humanity and its *reality*. The mushroom cloud is as *unreal* as it gets, because it is far away and gone, hopefully never to be repeated, while the kiss is real and repeatable, a reminder of the sweetness of family life and the continuation of peaceful existence. Here the soldier holds tightly a young woman and not a gun, gladly replacing the former for the latter.

The bottom two images shift us from some of the war consequences to the war's actual toll. On the right bottom, we see rows
of dead sailors carefully shrouded and bound on a ship, prepared
for burial at sea in the tropical waters of the South Pacific. These
sailors will not experience passionate kisses of reunion, no post-war
future; they paid the ultimate price for America's freedom: their
lives. In return, they receive an anonymous finality of the ocean
depths, devoid of even a simple grave-marker in a military cemetery
back home. While the mushroom cloud is almost surreal and reveals
little of the personal tragedies of nuclear weaponry, the realism presented by rows of shrouded bodies is undeniable: these sailors are
not coming home; they are the heroes or martyrs who died defending their country. They might be like pilots who were shot down and
whose remains were never found.

The shrouded bodies remind us of the contemporary American
artist Christo and his wife who spent decades wrapping books and oil
drums, bridges and buildings, and even himself in red cloth. Their
projects shift from urban to natural environments, displacing their
art from museums to the outdoors, and entreating their viewers to
perceive their temporary installations as an aesthetic experience. In
wrapping all sorts of entities, the Christos have been concealing the
real and presenting it in a packaged form, alienated from its environment, pristine in its detachment, and colorful in its fabrication.
(Sassower & Cicotello 2000, ch. 4). Unlike the dramatic and colorful
wrapping of the Christos, the sailors' shrouds are white, uniform,
almost anonymous; only the captain's records will testify to the loss
and note who was there, and how they died in the line of duty.

Less personal even than that is the image of a pile of victims'
shoes outside the barracks of Dachau, as seen in the photograph
on the lower left. Taken by the liberators, as opposed to numerous photographs taken by Nazi soldiers, camp guards, and officers
throughout the campaign of the Final Solution, one can hardly
imagine what this is a pile *of*: Why would anyone collect the victims' shoes? What testimony do they provide in relation to those
who wore them and were gassed and incinerated? Does the image
create a more powerful symbol of lost lives than an actual image of

dead bodies or portraits of the victims themselves? Though abstract in some sense, this photograph depicts something to which we can all relate, something as simple as shoes. The enormity of the loss of six million Jews, millions of civilians and soldiers, resistance fighters and "unfit" people, such as homosexuals and gypsies, is difficult to fathom, so difficult in fact that some claim silence is the only way to understand and remember the victims of Nazi atrocities. Perhaps a relatively *abstract* image of a pile of shoes can serve as powerfully as the image of the nuclear bomb's mushroom cloud; perhaps this image does indeed say what thousands of words cannot.

Those who visit what is left of concentration camps see little to-day of what went on during the war; they see some markings on the ground of where barracks were; they see some newly constructed barbwires where the original ones were set; they may see the re-mains of a crematorium, or the rail tracks that brought the victims day and night for years, but not much more. And still the visitors are silent, awed by what they *don't see*, so that other images come to the fore, bringing back memories of the past. The atomic bombs and concentration camps of World War II define the contours of that war and encapsulate the extent to which this war was unlike any war that preceded it: its inhumanity shattered claims of cosmopolitan sophistication and the progress of civilization. Looked at together, the four images presented are confusing and troubling, and as such, they lack a coherent message of victory and liberation.

Vietnam War (1961–1975)

Just as World War II was our "greatest war," which defined Ameri-can military dominance and portrayed it as the guarantor of world peace and prosperity, so the Vietnam War was our worst nightmare. It was a war started by others, and one whose closure evaded the efforts of three successive presidential administrations. It was a war that caused domestic pain and upheaval, while political careers were made and unmade. As the four images attest here, mixed mes-sages were abundant: from attack helicopters on the top left to an execution on the top right, from the spraying of Agent Orange on unsuspecting "enemy" civilians to a controversial veterans' memorial. Can anyone summarize this war in simple terms? Can anyone explain what really happened there?

The depiction of American soldiers using superior weaponry and airborne equipment to fight, evacuate, rescue, and intimidate also alludes to the ground conditions under which this war was fought: a conventional military operation on one hand was confronted by guerilla warriors on the other. American soldiers were not lined up against their enemies as was done in the Civil War, but they were confronted by a strategy of the Viet Cong that defied simple labels and criteria of any just war theory: who is fighting whom? Who is a soldier, and therefore a combatant that can be justifiably killed, and who is a civilian that as a noncombatant should be spared? Strategic questions become moral ones, and as the image of an airplane spraying over the jungle illustrates, it is difficult to make those distinctions. Is it therefore justified to ignore the personal, face-to-face battlefield, and spray from above a faceless jungle, as if to *exterminate* those hiding behind the trees? The language of extermination got its footing under the Nazi horrors and was oddly enough carried out by Americans, the heroes of previous wars. This level of confusion or double-talk undermined any possible slogans of freedom and liberation, humanitarian aid, and manifest destiny.

The veterans' memorial says as much by what it does not say as by what it does. Two enormous black slabs list the names of the fallen (engraved); its scale is overwhelming, its silence deafening; its abstractness represents more than could be represented by human-scale figures of soldiers (which in fact has been erected at the site by those objecting to the memorial whose image we present here). What can we say about the Vietnam War a generation or two later? Have we learned anything from that experience? Has this war been a humbling experience never to be repeated elsewhere?

The image on the top right side of a public execution by a Vietnamese general provided a vivid illustration of the "banality of evil" (in Hannah Arendt's phrase, referring to Nazi atrocities of World War II). This image was among those used by anti-Vietnam protesters to argue about the inherent immorality of all wars and the immediate need to withdraw from Vietnam. It can be argued that American public opinion was galvanized around this particular image, and that every political debate of the time had to account for it as a symbol of war atrocities and the ambiguities of moral standards in wartime.

Afghanistan War (2001–)

Even if you know nothing of the war in Afghanistan, most people are aware of what happened on September 11th, 2001: the two World Trade Center's towers in New York City were hit by airplanes and more than three thousand civilians died within hours. The shock to the nation's psyche helped push the United States toward a fear-driven path of anger never experienced before. The Bush administration mustered its intelligence and military might to defend the nation by attacking first the Talibans in Afghanistan followed by the Iraq invasion as an accompanying strategy for fighting Islamic terrorism. What was shocking about the terrorist attack in New York was the fact that airplanes were not used, as they had been used in World War I or World War II, as a means of transporting bombs and soldiers, but rather as the bombs themselves. The impact of the airplane, loaded as it was with its own fuel, caused damage similar to what a large bomb could do.

As we observe in the top right photograph, helicopters are still useful in combat, where mobility in difficult terrain is necessary. The hilltops of Afghanistan provide the Talibans with ample opportunities for ambush and guerilla warfare, hiding in caves, and defying conventional strategies of mass destruction and frontal assault. Can we ever win under these circumstances? Although the terrain has changed, is this war much different from what we went through in Vietnam?

The romantic image of the girl playing in the field of poppy-seed flowers is both innocent and universal in its appeal. Any mother or father around the globe would capture such an image to crystallize the innocence of youth and the playfulness of children in nature. Only those who know about the Afghan economy and its historic reliance on the opium trade would make the connection between this image and what these fields yield. When juxtaposed against the lower right image of Taliban fighters, grenade-launcher in hand, surrounded by desert, we realize that perhaps the picture of innocence is not so innocent after all: the opium trade funds terrorist activities. Children playing in opium fields are shielding these terrorists from American air-bombing sorties. And the image of the terrorist, calm and calculating, ready to strike innocent civilians around the world, is linked, of course, to the image on the top left of the bombed twin towers.

For those comparing the quagmire of Vietnam to what may become the quagmire of Afghanistan, one difference is being highlighted: al-Qaeda is threatening America's domestic national security as opposed to our concern with South Vietnam being overtaken by North Vietnam. Our national security is at stake, and if one has doubts about it, 9/11 is a painful reminder to the contrary. Since this war is still being waged, there has been a radical shift in the tactics being deployed on the ground there, and the overall rationale and intended consequences are still being debated and revised.

The Two Iraq Wars (1990–1991, and 2003–)

The first Iraq War, Desert Storm, was transmitted through television newscasts day and night. The establishment of CNN, and eventually Fox News, made news-reporting a non-stop 24/7 undertaking rather than twice daily. Americans were glued to their television sets, watching the war unfold, seeing images like the one on the top left, where "smart bombs" were launched from as far away as Kuwait to hit targets inside Bagdad, hundreds of miles away. It was as if the war was fought on a video-game console, without any harm to our soldiers. We fought back the encroaching and imperialistic Iraqi army, defended our Arab, oil-producing allies, and along the way significantly decreased the threat of the Iraqi army. Our victory was complete, our casualties minimal, and our superior technologies of war were successfully tested.

The image on the right top is a reminder of the incomplete conclusion to the first Iraq War that was completed by the younger George W. Bush, toppling the dictator Saddam Hussein. The cult of personality was such that every public square and large billboard carried his image so as to remind his citizens that he should be feared and admired, worshipped and reelected. The weapons of mass destruction that were presumably the reason for attacking Iraq in 2003 were never found; but America had other reasons to *justify* its declaration of war (as seen in Just War Theory). The photograph of the scene depicted was staged. Eye-witness reports testify that the toppling was reenacted a couple of times with civilian crowds being brought into the square and asked to cheer at the appropriate moments, all for the benefit of Western journalists who could then transmit this symbolic image to audiences back home. The war was justified for the results it brought about: freedom and democracy in place of oppressive dictatorship.

The bottom two images represent, as we have seen in the images of previous wars, the toll exacted on our troops. Soldiers die or are maimed; coffins carry the remains of those who died in the line of duty, and nurses and physical therapists help injured soldiers learn to cope with their disabilities. Nothing has changed over time, only the circumstances of the pain and suffering. And the censorship of these images, especially when they might turn around public support for the war, is still alive in the most democratic nation in the world. Can the wounded and handicapped soldier ever live a normal life? Would this image make us think twice before sending soldiers to fight a war?

The literature on the two Iraq Wars is extensive, written by former policy makers, such as Haass (2009), who suggest that the first war was one "of necessity," while the current one is "of choice," as well as by others, such as Peter Galbraith, who suggest that the current war in Iraq is strengthening our enemies (2008), because our policies have turned out to be untenable. We make no claims to survey the literature, but simply mention its vast spectrum of opinions and recommendations.

Israeli-Palestinian Conflict (1948–)

The reason to examine a conflict (rather than outright war) far away from our national borders has become more apparent in light of recent American incursions into the Middle East. The Israeli-Palestinian conflict dates back to the British Mandate over this part of the world and its departure under the United Nations' terms of independence to the indigenous people. The partition plan or the "two-state solution" was rejected by both sides, and the ensuing conflict remains unresolved to this date. American sympathies for the plight of the Jewish refugees of World War II have been tested over the years due to its own foreign policy concerns in the region. Yasir Arafat, seen in the top left photograph with Kofi Annan, then the Secretary General of the UN, remains an emblem of the Palestinian quest for international recognition and legitimacy and the hopes of a Palestinian homeland. He was able to galvanize his own people, garner the support of other Arab nations and the humanitarian aid of countries around the world. His unshaven face and traditional head-covering (Kafia) became synonymous with Palestinian aspiration for independence and the defiance of an indigenous people who have a right for self-identification and national credentials.

Yet some called Arafat a terrorist, claiming that his refusal to grant Israel the right to exist as a nation is tantamount to a declaration of genocide. Parallel with Israeli leaders who carried out acts of terrorism against British colonial oppression, it has been argued that the only way to turn a terrorist into a freedom fighter and eventually into a statesman is by legitimating the cause and creating the conditions of statehood. In light of the multiple interpretations (that are also contradictory) of the military and political frameworks within which the two sides operate, we can observe the two images on the right, both the top and bottom one: the loving father with his two children is in fact a terrorist who posed for this video before blowing himself up as a suicide bomber and inflicting the kind of damage portrayed in the lower image of a falafel-stand in Tel Aviv. The cherubic faces, the smiles of normality, the cartoonlike background of the top image turn out to be harbingers of evil destruction, where deliberate killing is on the agenda. American observers have been awe-struck and speechless trying to fathom what would drive anyone to kill oneself in the name of an ideology, a religion, a cause.

The tranquil landscape of the Biblical territory also known as the West Bank is divided by a wall that stretches for miles on end, separating the Palestinian villages from the Israeli city centers on the coast of the Mediterranean. Hailed as the best weapon with which to fight suicide bombers and the threat to national security, this wall has been blamed for "Apartheid-like" treatment of Palestinians by Israel. The conflict is characterized as inhumane because soldiers control civilians, dictate their every move and impose restrictions and curfews at will. Is this a war? Isn't a war fought by one army against another? Is there a possible solution to the conflict? Is the solution a military or a political one? Must we still abide by von Clausewitz's line that "war is nothing but the continuation of policy with other means"? (1976, 7).

LIST OF IMAGES

(Images listed from top left clockwise, on two facing pages; for enlarged scale and in some cases for color images, see the Internet.)

Napoleonic Wars (1792–1815)

1. *Napoleon Crossing St. Bernard* (Jacques Louis David, 1801). Commissioned by Napoleon to celebrate his daring crossing of the Great St. Bernard Pass in the Alps to win victory against the Austrians in 1800. Although he crossed on a mule, Napoleon requested he "be portrayed calm upon a fiery horse."
Image Credit: Awesome Art.Biz.

2. *Napoleon at the Battle of Ratisbon* (Claude Gautherot, circa 1810). Romantic Era painting showing Napoleon having his "wounded" foot examined on the battlefield by the physician Dominique Larrey.

Image Credit: Awesome Art.Biz.

3. *Third of May, 1808* (Francisco Goya, 1814). Depiction of the shooting of citizens in retaliation for guerilla attacks against the French occupying forces of the Napoleonic Conquest of Spain. Painted on request of the Bourbon restoration in 1814 to celebrate the "most noble and heroic actions of our glorious insurrection against the tyrant (Napoleon) of Europe." Ironically, Goya, as an "Enlightenment intellectual," actually welcomed the change of regime brought by the initial French occupation.

Image Credit: AICT/Allan T. Kohl.

4. *Disasters of War: Fatal Consequences of the Bloody War in Spain Against Bonaparte.* (Francisco Goya, 1808–1814). An image from a series of etchings by Goya that records his observations and emotions of the conflict. Drawn during the period of the war but not published in his lifetime. The sequence starts with images of hand to hand combat and proceeds through rape and executions to images of mutilated bodies. The series, which most scholars agree was generated from actual events, emphasizes suffering, cruelty, and despair.

Image Credit: AICT/Allan T. Kohl.

American Civil War (1861–1865)

5. *Manassas (Bull Run) Battlefield* (Alfred Waud, 1861). Images from sketch artists were often the public's only glimpses of battlefield action, since shutter speeds of cameras in this period were too slow to capture unposed live action.

Image Credit: Courtesy of the National Archives and Records Administration.

6. *Incidents of War; The Harvest of Death* (Alexander Gardner, 1863). This "shocking" documentary image of the dead from the Gettysburg Battlefield made a powerful impression on the public as it and other brutally realistic photographs of the slain troops of

both sides in the Civil War served to dissolve the glamorous aura of the fighting.

Image Credit: Courtesy of the National Archives and Records Administration.

7. *Home of a Rebel Sharpshooter* (Alexander Gardner, 1863). A dead Confederate infantry soldier was moved to this particular area of the battlefield (the Devil's Den) and posed by the photographer as a sharpshooter.

Image Credit: Courtesy of the National Archives and Records Administration.

8. *Fortifications at the Manassas (Bull Run) Battlefield* (Mathew Brady, 1863). The camera angle enlarges the scale of the stacked cannonballs to a contemporary viewer unfamiliar with the actual size of these Civil War munitions.

Image Credit: Courtesy of the National Archives and Records Administration.

World War I (1914–1918)

9. *Over the Top* (October 1916). A military archives photograph taken of Canadian Battalion training for trench warfare in St. Pol, France. Going over the crest of the trenches behind an artillery barrage to engage the enemy in "no man's land," a devastated strip of dirt and blood between them and the German fortifications, was the typical engagement of opposing forces in this war. The carnage from this extended and deadly trench warfare which characterized the battlefield action of WWI resulted in casualties of millions of lives lost.

Image Credit: Courtesy of GWPDA, Inc.

10. *Infantry Using Flamethrowers* (circa 1916). A WWI-era photograph of German Infantry engaged in using the new flamethrower weaponry. The image was staged during training maneuvers and vignetted within a sepia-toned oval composition.

Image Credit: Courtesy of GWPDA, Inc.

11. *I Want You for U.S. Army* (John Montgomery Flagg, 1917). A WWI Army recruitment poster based on an earlier British design

but adapted to the iconic "Uncle Sam" image and used successfully during WWII as well.

Image Credit: Courtesy of the National Archives and Records Administration.

12. *Black Flags* (Rene Magritte, 1936). Mysterious flying machine images painted by the Surrealistic artist Magritte that are ambiguous in their implications for good or evil, menace or playfulness, in times of war.

Image Credit: Scottish National Gallery of Modern Art.

World War II (1939–1945)

13. *Kissing the War Goodbye* (Victor Jorgensen, 1945). A U.S. Navy photojournalist captures an American sailor kissing a young woman on V-J Day in Times Square (NY). The young woman reportedly said: "There was no way to know who he was, but I didn't mind because he was someone who had fought for me." An almost identical image (made famous because it was published in *Life* magazine) was captured by the photographer Alfred Eisenstaedt.

Image Credit: Courtesy of the National Archives and Records Administration.

14. *Atomic Bomb Cloud over Nagasaki, Japan* (August 9, 1945). The mushroom cloud from the atomic bomb dropped on Nagasaki, Japan. The bomb was nicknamed the "Fat Man" after Winston Churchill. Of the nearly 300,000 people living in the area, approximately 75,000 were killed and another 70,000 severely injured. This image was photographed from the observation plane of the bombing mission.

Image Credit: Courtesy of the National Archives and Records Administration.

15. *Burial at Sea* (1944). A group of dead sailors prepared for burial on the deck of a U.S. destroyer in the Pacific theater of WWII.

Image Credit: Courtesy of the U.S. Naval Archives.

16. *Dachau Concentration Camp* (May 1945). View of a large pile of victims' shoes outside the barracks of the Dachau concentration camp.

Image Credit: Courtesy of the U.S. Holocaust Memorial Museum.

Vietnam War (1961–1975)

17. *U.S. 1st Cavalry Division (Airmobile)* (1960s). Army helicopter providing support to ground troops in the jungles of Vietnam.
Image Credit: Courtesy of Hawaii Army Museum Society.

18. *Execution of a Viet Cong Prisoner* (Eddie Adams, February 1, 1968). Photograph of General Nguyen Ngoc Loan executing a Viet Cong prisoner accused of commanding an assassination platoon that targeted South Vietnamese police on the streets of Saigon in public view. This image became a defining image that started to change the American public's viewpoint on the war.
Image Credit: AP Photo/Adams.

19. *Chemical Defoliant Dispersal* (1965). Image of air dispersal over the rural areas of South Vietnam of the chemical defoliant "Agent Orange" which contained highly toxic dioxin. This spraying was an attempt to deprive the enemy of their forest cover and food supply.
Image Credit: Courtesy of Hawaii Army Museum Society.

20. *Vietnam War Veterans' Memorial* (Maya Lin, 1982). Simple Walls of Black granite sited below ground level and inscribed with the names of the dead comprise this somber and beloved memorial to the veterans of the Vietnam War.
Image Credit: Courtesy of the National Parks Service.

Afghanistan War (2001–)

21. *World Trade Center Attacked* (September 11, 2001). Image of the suicide highjacked aircraft attack on the two towers of the World Trade Center initiated by the terrorist organization al-Qaeda under the leadership of Osama bin Laden. The Twin Towers collapsed due to the effects of the fires started by the collisions, killing approximately 3,000.
Image Credit: Courtesy of DHD Multimedia Gallery/Anonymous.

22. *Fighting in the Tora Bora* (2002). Elite Special Forces units fighting in the craggy mountainous area of Eastern Afghanistan known as Tora Bora where the enemy al-Qaeda and its leader

Osama bin Laden were hidden in an intricate complex of caves and *supported* by regional tribal leaders.

Image Credit: AP Photo/Thorne.

23. *Taliban Fighters* (circa 2002). Battlefield image of two Taliban fighters posed with a deadly RPG. Their faces covered for anonymity and disguise of their combatant status.

Image Credit: AP Photo/Khan.

24. *Afghan Poppy Field* (circa 2004). Afghanistan child photographed in the opium poppy fields in bloom. Cultivation of opium poppies sustains much of the rural economy of this country.

Image Credit: AP Photo/Butler.

Iraq War (1990–1991, and 2003–)

25. *Smart Bombing of Baghdad* (Television Image, 2001). Smart bombing campaign of Baghdad photographed at night during the first Iraq campaign and televised to the world. Desert Storm was the name of the war, and "Shock and Awe" was the name of the strategy that used overwhelming invasion forces.

Image Credit: AP Photo/Mollard.

26. *Saddam Hussein Statue Toppled in Baghdad* (April 9, 2001). The toppling of the landmark statue of Saddam Hussein in Firdos Square (central Baghdad) and a cheering crowd of Iraqis shortly after the arrival of U.S. Marine forces. This was a staged event that carefully controlled the perimeter of the square and those admitted to witness the destruction of the monument.

Image Credit: AP Photo/Delay.

27. *Coffins of Iraq War Casualties* (2004). Flag-shrouded coffins of U.S. casualties from Iraq War in cargo hold of transport aircraft. The Bush administration tried to limit access of these images to the public and they were never "officially" released.

Image Credit: Courtesy of the U.S. Air Force.

28. *Iraq War Amputee in College* (2007). Kevin Blanchard, George Washington University student, shown in his dorm-room, is one of the many Iraq War wounded with amputated limbs due to the frequency and effectiveness of the roadside bombing techniques of

the enemy. His return from the war initiated a "new war," struggling with bureaucracies and daily life.

Image Credit: Courtesy of Nick Gingold/The GW Hatchet.

Israeli-Palestinian Conflict (1948–)

29. *Arafat and Annan Meet in Gaza* (October 2000). Kofi Annan, Secretary General of the United Nations, meets with Yasir Arafat, President of the Palestinian National Authority in Gaza, in an effort to defuse the long-standing conflict with the Israelis.

Image Credit: AP Photo/Hussein.

30. *Palestinian Suicide Bomber* (2006). Image of a Palestinian suicide bomber from his farewell video, holding his two young children.

Image Credit: AP Photo/HO.

31. *Tel Aviv Suicide Bombing Aftermath* (April 2006). Aftermath of a suicide bombing attack on a falafel restaurant in Tel Aviv, Israel that killed 9 and wounded over 70 civilians. The Islamic Jihad claimed responsibility for the attack.

Image Credit: AP Photo/Kami.

32. *West Bank Security Barrier* (2009). A view of a section of the "security barrier" Israel is constructing along its 365 kilometer West Bank border with Palestine in an effort to control suicide bombing excursions into its territory. Opponents call it an "Apartheid Wall."

Image Credit: Courtesy of Brian Carroll.

3

RECAPTURING REALITY

REPRESENTING THE REALITIES OF WAR

As we have argued in the first chapter, the stakes are quite high when a country is engaged in warfare: soldiers die, civilians die, and a great deal of destruction takes place. The motivation to engage in war may remain in dispute, critical geo-political analysis may still continue, but once troops are mobilized and the first shots are fired, the way to maintain or stop a war depends as much on public sentiment as on the actual arguments presented by generals and politicians. If the public can stomach a war, then it will proceed; when the public is eager to punish an alleged enemy or exact revenge, funding for warfare will be readily available; but when the public is unconvinced or even critical of a military engagement, political leaders lose their positions, and generals are asked to resign or retire. In short, public opinion in approving or disproving of a potential or an ongoing war is a crucial variable in its initiation and execution. It is with this in mind that we move to consider how the public, and especially a contemporary public exposed to a constant barrage of media images, can be or more often is being manipulated in one way or the other. The potential or "anticipated" reading of the images becomes an important and even crucial factor in constructing and justifying the arguments in this visual "battle." The battle is ultimately for the approval or disapproval of war policies in the public's mind, as happened, for instance, in the 1960s and 1970s with certain Vietnam War images. We recall the images of Vietnamese children fleeing napalm bombs, the victims of the My Lai massacre lying on the roadside, and the one included in chapter 2 of the execution on the streets of Saigon.

Re-presenting reality is an activity fraught with dangers even when we are judicious about making sure to present every aspect and detail of reality. Since the best we can do is bracket a portion of reality, a segment of the fabric of facts, we are inherently engaged in an act of selection: making choices of what to foreground and what to leave as the background, what to focus on and what to overlook, in short, what to highlight. In the process, we are making decisions, and these decisions, however honorable and innocent, or accidental and inadvertent, may turn out to distort the entire picture or image of reality. This is true when we paint a landscape scene and when we shoot a photograph or a video of a street or a concert. Without getting too involved in all the psycho-social intricacies of artists and their personal biographies, we can readily admit that the inherent problems of aesthetic re-presentation are such that they require a careful outline or analysis of the *criteria* according to which *artistic choices* are made, whether they are, for example, for ornamental purposes or journalistic in character. Since the journalistic stakes in the case of warfare are more crucial for public policy purposes because of the veracity claimed on their behalf, let us revisit the images presented in chapter 2, and observe, in general, how one could be *reading* them from modernist and postmodernist perspectives. The distinction, as we mentioned in chapter 1, is crucial insofar that the former is bound by a stricter set of criteria that allow for a relatively simple deconstruction, while the latter remains purposefully open-ended and thereby empowers the observer to come up with whatever reading is contextually appropriate (or not). In there, of course, lies the problem: is the viewer really endowed with such powers of discernment and judgment? Or is the whole process already set up in one particular way or another?

As we go over the eight wars (in sixteen pages) depicted in chapter 2, we must remind the reader that this is not an exercise in history or art history, but rather a philosophically minded examination of how history is treated in the case of wars. It should also be mentioned that other wars or conflicts could have been used to illustrate our points, and that our own choice has more to do with general public familiarity than with anything special about these wars themselves. For example, we could have used the American-Mexican War (1846–1848), the Spanish Civil War (1936–1939), the Korean War (1950–1953), and many others in which the United States had some involvement. Perhaps one significant factor in our selection is the introduction of photography as a medium of image producing, one that is easily reproduced and distributed across print news media. Photography complicates the discussion over the *reality* that is being re-presented (as opposed to the obviously *staged* [painted or sculpted] images of warriors and generals). We see that each two-page collage provides a broader and perhaps a more accurate picture of the war because four images can represent more aspects and details of the war than a single one. Yet, one can argue that each war could have been represented with one image, an image that captures the imagination, and one that explains, so to speak, everything! This would be the case, for example, with one (of many) canonical image of World War II of the liberation of Europe by American troops, where a tank or a row of tanks meanders through narrow village streets and beautiful women wave their hands and throw flowers at the handsome soldiers who smile triumphantly back at them. Likewise, a single image of the mushroom cloud of the atomic bombs dropped on Hiroshima and Nagasaki could say more about the essence of the war and the introduction of nuclear warfare into the global arena than any particular photograph of this or that battle. Some would say that the American troops landing on the shores of France on D-day, for example, symbolizes our involvement in the war and our rescue of the Europeans from the clutches of fascism.

The conviction that it is possible to sum up reality with one image that speaks for everything results from a modernist perspective, since it has been the common perception that a picture is worth a thousand words. There is a sense, perhaps because of Nietzsche's notion of perspective—that the perspective from which we view something affects how we see it—that the vision we have is both objective and transparent, that it can transcend the perspective itself and stand for and capture the entire entity that is being observed. The fact that Nietzsche also believed that there are multiple perspectives (and therefore the entity under observation may be seen differently from diffcrent perspectives) does not undermine the modernist commitment to provide a perfect and transparent vision, one that can be comprehended by all. Nietzsche himself, though an artist in more than one sense, has this to say about the artist's sense of truth or adherence to a strict representation of reality:

> In regard to knowledge of truths, the artist possesses a weaker morality than the thinker; he does not want to be deprived of the glittering, profound interpretations of life and guards against simple and sober methods and results. He appears to be fighting on behalf of the greater dignity and significance of man; but in reality . . . he thus considers the perpetuation of his mode of creation more important than scientific devotion to the true in any form, however plainly this may appear. (Nietzsche 1977, 125)

As seen from Nietzsche's perspective, there is indeed a *scientific* way of seeing things, of recording the facts, of reaching a consensus about what is *true*. The artists, though, modernist or not, remain beholden to their chosen profession, and in its name will interpret the truth. A modernist may pick one image and draw from it all the facts necessary to assess the war and elicit a particular sentiment from the viewer. A modernist look at each image would include all the details related to the artist, David or Goya, as the case may be, and the kind of political affiliation or ideological commitments they have in portraying the Napoleonic Wars as either heroic and beneficial or as cruel and devastating, so as to be able to distinguish these personal opinions or biases from the facts about the war. A modernist may also insist on seeing all the available images in order to have a full picture of the war, and thus would have to weigh the success against the suffering, and with some kind of social, political, and economic book-keeping summarize a utilitarian argument in favor or against the war. A modernist, in short, will undermine the leeway given to artists to provide their own interpretations of the true nature of this or that war.

A postmodernist, by contrast, would argue that no comprehensive picture is ever available (whether one relies on Nietzsche or not), and as such one is justified in focusing on one image, and one image alone, to assess from a particular perspective the Napoleonic Wars. In doing so, the postmodernist would discard the obvious propagandistic image of the heroic Napoleon (David's), and suggest that any paid artist can depict anyone as well or better than a hero really is in person, and thus improve on the image for popular consumption. Obviously the payment to the artist prejudices the work, and as such the image can never be considered *real* or *objective*. Put differently, while the modernist confines the viewing to the framed image itself (and tries to appreciate *the inner logic* of the situation), the postmodernist looks around the framed image (and tries to figure out the broader context of the image and *what is excluded*). Similarly, a focus on one of Goya's images must be construed from the particular perspective and context of the defeated Spanish, and because of this perspective, the best judgment one can make is limited and subjective. The postmodernist would be considering as many factors as the modernist has, and in doing so would work through a similar process of assessment. What would differentiate the modernist and the postmodernist is the very notion that a *definitive picture* of the wars is tenable at all. And if one were to pursue such an undertaking, both would insist on knowing under what conditions and with what criteria it was accomplished. So, the enumeration of facts and dates, images and testimonies, based on a solid foundation of how evidence is gathered, and what makes testimonies credible, leads the modernist to a point in which a judgment is not only made but can be *justified*. For the modernist there is a process that *legitimates a judgment* about an image and its relation to reality. By contrast, the postmodernist must remain *skeptical and critical* about the facts, images, and the foundations themselves. The foundations are not as solid as initially conceived, and as such can lead to misrepresentations that are inevitably partial, subjective, prejudicial, and idiosyncratic.

The American Civil War, more than any other war before it, brought to the civilian population images from the front, and therefore engaged the public in the conflict. When newspapers are distributed around the country with certain photographs on the front page, people see them and ask questions. In later wars, movie and television cameras were sent to the front. Newsreels came to audiences in movie theaters and later to home audiences on television sets. The immediacy of the war could not be avoided. How much to show, what to show, and how often, are questions that political and military leaders still struggle with as they invite or bar journalists from the battlefields. As much as we believe in the freedom of the press, we also believe that national security questions trump journalist access. Consequently, there is a delicate balance that must be maintained and that is constantly being contested between *complete* and *censored* access to military activities during wars. The public seems to keep its own delicate balance between wanting to know everything about the war and wanting to be shielded from its atrocities, as we are seeing our own behavior during the current war in Iraq. Images of the torture at the Abu-Ghraib prison in Baghdad did more damage to American interests around the world than anything else we might have done. It was not the torture per se that upset viewers, but the revelation of the callousness with which soldiers treated other human beings, the way one culture looked down and mocked another, and this illuminated American hypocrisy (claiming to be humanitarian while treating some people as sub-humans).

Though we provided some analyses of the images in chapter 2, we are aware that other analyses would be just as valid. There could be many more interpretations, many more points of view from which to *read* these images. There are cases, as one can see in the four images of the Israeli-Palestinian Conflict, where one can construct a *linear narrative*, moving from the top left to the top right and then down to the lower right and onto the lower left: Arafat set Palestinian identity in historical terms that required the kind of suicide bombers to blow up the enemy that stood in its way to full recognition as a legitimate state, and the only way to stop this kind of civilian killing is by erecting a wall of separation between the Israelis and the Palestinians. One image leads to the next, one explanation makes sense of its predecessor; and in this way all the points are linked into one coherent fabric. This kind of reading would be more difficult with other four images of the wars we collected. More information might be needed, and more information would bring about more points of view, and more points of views might be conflicting and not necessarily complementary. The more you know about the image, the more you realize that your first *take* was superficial and misleading, and even dangerously so.

For example, a pastoral image might be in fact an image of pain and despair, a Christo-like image of wrapping (World War II) is in fact an image of a group of dead sailors about to be buried at sea, as we mentioned in chapter 2. Should the reader have this information in order to appreciate the image? Does it contribute to or detract from the reading or appreciation of the image? Should images stand *on their own* and thereby demand a framing by their creators that gives sufficient information to the observer, no matter what personal background is brought to the viewing? The facts end up crushing the prefigured ideas we might have, and the wishful thinking we bring to the *aesthetic experience* of watching: instead of soothing and inspiring, inspiring and sublime, we might be upset and confused. But facts, as we know by now, are themselves problematized in their apprehension and comprehension, because, to use the scientific literature for a moment, all observations are *theory-laden* (Hanson 1965). This means that the theories we study and believe in before we even collect one bit of data or fact are bound to inform our collection and as such would enable us to collect some facts and not see others, so that the process of data collection or fact finding is itself compromised. For example, when you were first asked by your teacher to describe what you *saw* through a microscope, you probably saw nothing. But when your teacher was more precise in asking you if you see this or that particular dot, all of a sudden you saw it! What happened? The dot was there all along, but once you were informed what to expect, you were able to see it. Artistic images are no different and suffer from the same kind and level of indeterminacy as scientific facts: we are informed what to see and how to see it.

War images play a crucial role in determining how the "road to war" (or as it is more commonly referred to, the "road to peace") is perceived by the general public. Political careers and military support depend on this perception, as we have argued before. We can represent the two Iraq Wars either as a linear progression from one to the other, or as two distinct wars with different agendas and, of course, different results. The first war, "Desert Storm," was characterized in terms of the physical distance from the enemy so that military engagement and destruction were a palatable strategy on the road to Kuwaiti liberation and regional peace. The second war, which continues to this date, was originally set in motion on the road to Baghdad, traversed with personnel carriers and tanks, and within three weeks obliterated the Iraqi army. The first road led to a relative calm back home, with congratulatory smiles about "smart bombs" and precision-destruction, all shown daily on the major television networks. The second road has led to numerous controversies, some related to the image of President Bush's landing on an aircraft carrier with a heroic smile (a modern Napoleon?), and some related to torture in prisons (censored just like in the Civil War). Perhaps in both cases we are discussing the "road to democracy," a road traditionally understood in ideological senses, some militant (wars of independence) and some peaceful (Gandhi's non-violent resistance). It is an image of the American colonies fighting their way to freedom from the British crown; the South Africans fighting for freedom and equality against Apartheid policies; and the Iraqis pitted against each other and definitely in opposition to a so-called imperial American incursion into their land to dominate their political institutions. Is this, indeed, a road to democracy, or a road to more pain and suffering, more civil strife, and more hatred of America? The fact of the matter is that political and ideological questions are raised by war images, whether we like it or not.

It is not as if torture is foreign in wars or that torture has not produced valuable information in every war; but seeing it brings the issue to the front, and brings about the kind of questions we usually avoid asking. It is not merely that images are more powerful than words or that the reality of images is more frightening than the reality itself, due to its power to recall and reframe that which was ignored or justified at the moment. Rather, it is the public accessibility to these images that opens a discussion and forces a more open debate where before military and political censorship could halt any scrutiny or critique. More than one hundred and fifty years ago, the art world heralded the use of photography as the shift to a broader skilled community that could thereby join the artistic community, and be more *real* in its depiction (however much this notion has been contested since then); nowadays, with an inexpensive digital camera or cell-phone any enlisted soldier or civilian bystander can transmit images through the Internet literally to the entire world, surpassing the standard controls of news agencies and military censors. Is this an improvement? Is the pain worth the truth? How can you and should you read war images? Is it indeed your patriotic and civic duty to read war images? Nietzsche's warning about the artistic *creation* remains a useful reminder about the production of images, the *fabrication* of images. This creation and fabrication, this process of putting together and building up an image should alert us to the process of selection, the decision-making method used by image makers. From this perspective, then, we suggest that we are first and foremost modernist readers and consumers of images, and only later become postmodernist interpreters of images: we are drawn to a definitive closure that an image provides (cropped, framed, and staged), yet remain uneasy if this closure is justified (what is the background story, the context, the alternative perspective?).

THE PREDICAMENT OF JUST WAR THEORIES

We have been arguing that contemporary perceptions of wars are bound by war images. Whether they provide *closure* or open a *critical discussion* remains open for debate. But what is clear to us is that war images inform and influence public opinion and eventually public policy regarding wars. Carl von Clausewitz, one of the foremost war theorists, in his book *The Principles of War*, reminds us that "warfare has three main objects: (a) To conquer and destroy the armed power of the enemy; (b) To take possession of his material and other sources of strength, and (c) To gain public opinion" (Von Clausewitz 2003, 45). How does one "gain public opinion"? Is it solely in terms of great victories, as he says? Or is it by preserving a higher moral ground than the enemy's? Public opinion, as we have argued all along, is primarily influenced by war images and their dissemination through proper military and political channels. Our focus on war images, then, is part and parcel of our understanding of how wars are perceived and supported, and how they are promoted or condemned, how they are fought and brought to an end. Regardless of the actual success in the battlefield, as most military historians and theorists would agree, if the public back home refuses to support a war, it is bound to fail sooner or later. Financial funding will be curtailed; less civilians will volunteer to serve as soldiers; and political leaders will lose their thirst for revenge, for example, and call back the generals and their armies. In short, where the people are sovereign, their opinions count. Sun Tzu, the ancient Chinese general, agreed that "in war, the general receives his commands from the sovereign" (Sun Tzu 2002, 64). Admittedly the sovereign of his day was an emperor and not a democratic body politic, but nonetheless it was understood that political leaders controlled their militaries, and if a political cause was not fulfilled, then there was no purpose to fighting a war. Even an emperor needed to be convinced that a war was winnable, and that the reports from the battlefield were reliable. Likewise, in some Native American tribes, the declaration of war could be undertaken by the men, but women had the veto power to withhold support, such as food supplies, since, the logic went, they would bear the brunt of disaster in case of the war's failure (Mays 2004, 78). One recalls also Aristophanes' *Lysistrata* (412 BCE) in which occurs the absurd possibility that women would call a "sexual strike" in order to stop both sides, Athens and Sparta, from continuing their war. Absurd and shocking as it appears in the play, Aristophanes was searching for a way to point out the futility of wars and what may remain the only way men would listen to reason: the denial of sexual favors.

When speaking of wars, we should recall the rich history of warfare and what has been written about it. This is a worthwhile exercise so as to define the moral contours of the war, the social context from which it arises, and the intimate relations between civilians and warriors. As Lionel Giles reminds us, "written about 500 B.C., *The Art of War* by Sun Tzu is the oldest military treatise in the world" (Sun Tzu 2002, 9). As such, the words of its author retain their power today: "The art of war is of vital importance to the state. It is a matter of life and death, a road either to safety or to ruin. Hence it is a subject of inquiry which can on no account be neglected" (Ibid., 40).

Sun Tzu was a Chinese general who wanted to ensure the practical training of soldiers, and who also understood how important warfare was to the well-being of a state. Can a state hope to survive without having a military? Can a military prevail against encroaching enemies without proper training? And can training ever be effective without developing principles and frameworks for strategies and tactics? With these questions in mind, Sun Tzu proceeded, testing his own ideas in the fields of battle.

In 1521, the great Italian political theorist and counsel, Niccolo Machiavelli, wrote *The Art of War*. Not only does he agree in principle with Sun Tzu about the importance of warfare studies, he is quick to explain that one's behavior as a civilized citizen and as a soldier is not that different, and moreover, that one complements the other:

> For all the arts that have been introduced into society for the common benefit of mankind, and all the ordinances that have been established to make them live in fear of God and in obedience to human laws, would be vain and insignificant if they were not supported and defended by a military force; this force, when properly led and applied, will maintain those ordinances and keep up their authority, although they perhaps may not be perfect or flawless. But the best ordinances in the world will be despised and trampled under foot when they are not supported, as they ought to be, by a military power. (Machiavelli 1965, 4)

Machiavelli, like Sun Tzu, appreciated the importance of a military power that under the right training and application of force can support civic institutions. Civilian life, however perfect in its design, cannot survive or thrive without a military. This reliance on military forces to ensure the domestic obedience to laws further enhances the power of the state to withstand attacks by foreign powers, as far as Machiavelli was concerned. If one were to challenge Machiavelli's view in its narrow focus on princes and petty-dictators (the Medici family or the Popes, for example, in Italy), there is a ready answer to this challenge: national security. Even the greatest democracies must rely on state secrets and national security networks to bolster the defenses of their countries and ensure internal compliance and peace.

By the time we reach the nineteenth century, the definitive works most commonly cited are those written by the German general and military theorist Carl von Clausewitz. Having acknowledged the congruence between political and military aims, and having realized how one defines and motivates the other, von Clausewitz was careful to explain the limitations of war theory in the face of an actual war (Von Clausewitz 2007, 17; see also 89). He continues to explain that "warfare thus eludes the strict theoretical requirements that extremes of force be applied" (Ibid., 19). One must follow one's judgment, and the law of probability becomes the standard by which action is undertaken. As much as von Clausewitz is concerned with providing a framework for warfare and a set of principles to be studied, he is also aware of their limitations. The human element must be considered:

> Although our intellect always longs for clarity and certainty, our nature finds uncertainty fascinating . . . it must also take the human factor into account. . . . The art of war deals with living and with moral forces. Consequently, it cannot attain the absolute, or certainty; it must always leave a margin for uncertainty, in the greatest things as much as in the smallest. (Ibid., 27)

Once the "human factor" is taken into account, and we realize not only that a theoretical exercise is futile in the face of the reality of war, but also that we have to consider humans, the entire enterprise of discussing and analyzing warfare becomes more complicated, perhaps even more messy and contradictory. There is a "paradoxical trinity—composed of primordial violence, hatred, and enmity," according to von Clausewitz, "which are to be regarded as a blind natural force" (Ibid., 30). By associating the first of these, primordial violence, with the people, the second with the commander and his army, and the third with the government, von Clausewitz suggests that passions have as much to do with warfare as discipline or obedience to orders. In order to make sense of his own war experiences and those of others, and in order to be able to instruct future generations of warriors, von Clausewitz introduces what he calls a "critical analysis" to the entire enterprise (Ibid., 106), a practice which will be covered more extensively in the next chapter. In the meantime, we'd like to pay closer attention to the idea that "primordial" passions are invoked in the name of war, to either frighten or motivate soldiers and civilians alike.

When we return to examining the psychology of war, we may realize that, according to Lawrence LeShan,

> When we go to war, our perception of reality—of what we are and what is happening in the world around us—is quite different from that which we commonly use in peacetime. This shift, when it occurs, makes war much more difficult to prevent, or to stop once it has started. (LeShan 2002, 3)

LeShan reiterates what we have said all along, that there are multiple perspectives from which reality is perceived. What is startling in his observation is the comfort zone we inhabit once we shifted into the *war zone.* It is as if we enter the twilight zone and all bets are off: we have no idea what is going to happen next. According to LeShan, there have been historically three basic theories that relate to the *causes* of wars:

1. That war was inevitable given the nature of man; that all men had a basic instinct to acquire power, and this led inevitably to war.

2. That wars were fought for economic gain.
3. That man was a group animal, and that the nature and structure of groups led inevitably to wars. (Ibid., 6)

As you can tell from these three theories, there is something *inevitable* about wars, whether the causes are related to individual drives or group behavior. Arthur Koestler is cited as claiming that "men fight wars for reasons of group identification and loyalty" (Ibid., 7), especially in the face of a common enemy that pulls them together. We can recall in this context the Bible, where wars are constantly fought by the Israelites in order to conquer land, to bring about monotheism, and to fulfill God's promise to Abraham and Moses, and eventually to Jesus and Muhammad. Religious wars or religiously motivated wars (about which we shall have more to say in the next chapter) have been based to a large extent on these psychological prototypes discussed here. How does one pull a group of nomads together? How can we distinguish one clan from another? How does one ensure the development of personal identity within a group?

LeShan continues to explain the psycho-social dynamics of participation in wars: "Certainly what war promises differs from what it delivers. Nevertheless it does deliver temporary solutions to psychological problems for a very large percentage of the population. And once a war begins the social pressures to continue it are very strong" (Ibid., 29). So, the dual notions of personal identification and group cohesion are important once a war has begun. What is frightening is the level to which "social pressures" make a critical evaluation and strategic assessment difficult to articulate in public. The *logic* of this social process and peer pressure is described in more detail, as LeShan alerts us to the "ideas" that signal a movement towards war:

1. The idea that there is a particular enemy nation that embodies evil, *and that if it were defeated, the world would become paradise.* (It is the latter part of this statement that is crucial as a danger signal. The first part may be true—as with Tamerlane's hordes or Hitler's Germany.)

2. The idea that taking action against this enemy (now *the enemy*) is the path to glory and to legendary heights of existence.
3. The idea that anyone who does not agree with this accepted wisdom is a traitor. (Ibid., 30)

The group psychology that evolves along these lines, along these ideas, pulls society into a cohesive monolith without the benefit of critical objection: you are either with us or against us! And if you are not with us, you are a "traitor." And while there were times when you could be ignorant of a war, technology has made wars more accessible so that the public feels more personally engaged in the wars, even when they are fought far away. With the advent of photography, especially in the Civil War, "it was neither sweet nor fitting to die for one's country" (Ibid., 60–61).

But, as LeShan admits, it is not only about the technologies of war or the ways in which they are portrayed back home; it is just as much about the *perspective* from which these images are conveyed to the general public eagerly engaged in the war, awaiting yet another story of heroism to pull the group (nation) together. He gives an excellent example of how our perceptions have changed in regards to heroic self-sacrifice in the case of American versus Japanese pilots who dove their airplanes into naval vessels:

> During World War II, Captain Colin Kelly was widely reported to be a great American hero for sinking a Japanese battleship by diving his airplane down her funnel. He never actually did this, but we needed a hero and the story was useful at the time. When the Japanese began using kamikaze tactics toward the end of the war, however, Kelly's name abruptly disappeared from public mention. After all, if Kelly was a hero for what he had done, then so were the Japanese suicide pilots, and we could not have that. (Ibid., 62)

This double standard by which we measure the same act is mentioned in this context in terms of hero-worship, and the need to have an iconic image, even if false or staged, in order to bring about social cohesion. Yet, in another context, this double standard is understood to be a contradictory assessment of one's action or behavior, depending, as it always does, on whose perspective is valued more or given more credence: can there be a moral equivalence between an American and a Japanese pilot? If one is a hero on a suicide mission, can the other be honored in a similar fashion? In other words, seeing an image of a pilot diving into a naval battleship alone does not tell the whole story, because the circumstances and intent of the action must be accounted for as well. (Incidentally, there are Internet sites that claim that the *real hero* was in fact Captain Richard E. Fleming and not Captain Colin Kelly.)

As we recall the images of the eight wars we described in chapter 2, we should note that LeShan has classified them in his own way. He distinguishes between what he calls "mythic wars" and "sensory wars," so as to highlight positive elements associated with the former and the negative ones associated with the latter category. For him the Civil War and the two World Wars were mythic insofar as they elicited a sense of excitement and heroism as well as a sense that these wars would bring about a new and better world order. By contrast, the Korean, Vietnam, and Persian Gulf wars elicited "sad and regretful feelings" (Ibid., 66–67). LeShan's classifications and judgments may differ from what was discussed in chapter 2, yet serve as useful examples of how different people perceive wars differently. As much as LeShan insists on his classification and the great differences associated with the feelings soldiers and civilians have towards wars, he still suggests an underlying "elements of human motivations toward war":

1. Displacement of aggression
2. Projection of self-doubts and self-hatred.
3. Lack of meaning and purpose in life.
4. A need for greater belonging to a group. (Ibid., 73)

There is something seductive about this list of basic or primordial emotions of humans, as if this were a *universal* foundation of human nature that promotes warfare. Just as we speculated in *Political Blind Spots* (2006) about a universal language of art that transcends national boundaries and found that hypothesis problematic, we might view LeShan's claims to be problematic. Do all humans have an innate aggression they need to "displace"? Do we all exhibit some form of "self-hatred" and are therefore prone to attempt the killing of other human beings like us? Is the only way to find "meaning and purpose in life" through warfare? Why is gardening not enough? And finally, can we find no other way to belong "to a group" other than through warfare?

These questions may seem rhetorical or unanswerable, yet they are worthy questions to ask; they are the questions we must contemplate when a universal claim about aggression is proposed. If we find no alternative answers, we may end up along side LeShan claiming that "war is very attractive to human beings" (Ibid., 117). How can anyone suggest that there is something "attractive" about wars? How can anyone intimate that killing is somehow "attractive"? We must credit LeShan for ending his book with a set of recommendations that attempt to educate us to "celebrate" ourselves as individuals and "contribute" to our communities in ways other than fighting wars. He recommends ways through which we can become more helpful to each other and less aggressive, ways through which our learning processes can provide prosperity and peaceful coexistence (Ibid., 119). But his initial arguments about the human traits that *inevitably* bring about wars remain intact: wishful thinking is not going to make them go away.

Let's reconsider what must go through a pilot's mind (the Japanese Kamikaze) so as to commit suicide by flying his plane into a ship. Is the glory of Japan worth the sacrifice? Has his life no meaning and is therefore dispensable? Would the emperor's gratitude, perhaps his mere acknowledgment, make this ultimate gesture of obedience worthy of one's afterlife honor? A psychological explanation might end up with a characterization of a pathology, a sickness of sorts that is rooted in the pilot's sense of worthlessness. Do soldiers feel this way? Do they only feel this way during wars? But if we recall all the great war theorists who have commented on the shift from being a civilian to being a soldier, we may stop for another set of reflections. First, some countries have mandatory conscription, which means that every citizen must serve in the military for a set length of time (Germany, Israel, Switzerland, Brazil, Russia, for example), while others have a voluntary military in which only some citizens serve (the United States). In the former case, there is fluidity between one role and the other, so that the mental *shift* in perspective between a civilian and a soldier is relatively smooth. In the latter case, it can be argued, the professionalization of military personnel may transform them into mercenaries whose mission is to engage in wars (rather than reluctantly respond to their initiation).

Second, the very engagement in acts of war, which speaking plainly is the act of killing other people, is morally problematic. The seventh Commandment specifically forbids us from killing, not to mention deliberately murdering other people. Civic law has made provisions for different kinds of killing, from first-degree murder (premeditated killing), to killing in self-defense, to manslaughter, and accidents. The nuances we appreciate in our interactions with others allow us to distinguish between what is morally wrong and therefore punishable by law, from what is morally neutral and therefore forgiven. The realities of warfare obliterate at times those fine moral and legal distinctions; they don't enjoy the slow deliberation of philosophers and lawyers; they require an immediate response, one that must be decisive if it is to be effective at all.

As mentioned in chapter 1 when discussing *just war theory*, there are cases in which wars are justified and cases when they are not. Likewise, there are arguments to be made to justify the declaration of wars, and arguments to justify specific methods of warfare. One can justifiably enter a war, but fight it unjustly; one can be mistaken in entering a war (e.g., use false intelligence that justified declaring war), but be just in fighting it. The central issue, as Walzer so aptly suggests, is that all of these arguments are moral in nature, and as moral arguments they require careful critical analysis of the terms that are being used and the examples that explain them (Walzer 1977, preface). Walzer reminds us that "moral discourse is always suspect, and war is only an extreme case of the anarchy of moral meanings" (Ibid., 11). Regardless of the ambiguities of moral definitions and the interpretations of moral principles, Walzer also suggest that "the truth is that one of the things most of us want, even in war, is to act or to seem to act morally. And we want that, most simply, because we know what morality means (at least, we know what it is generally thought to mean)" (Ibid., 20). Though similarly suggestive of a universal principle, this view differs from LeShan's psychological view insofar as the common denominator is morality rather than an aggressive element in human nature. As such, this view offers hope for resolution, even a potential for pragmatic policies, as we shall discuss in the next chapter.

Although Walzer's original text was meant as a response to the Vietnam War and the debates that ensued after its conclusion, he has since remained involved in assessing wars and conflicts around the globe. Collaborating with Avishai Margalit, Walzer summarizes his view of just war theory in the following way:

> The point of just war theory is to regulate warfare, to limit its occasions, and to regulate its conduct and legitimate scope. Wars between states should never be total wars between nations or people. Whatever happens to the two armies involved, whichever one wins or loses, whatever the nature of the battles or the extent of the casualties, the two nations, the two peoples, must be functioning communities at the war's end. The war cannot be a war of extermination or ethnic cleansing. And what is true for states is also true for state-like political bodies such as Hamas and Hezbollah, whether they practice terrorism or not. The people they represent or claim to represent are a people like any other. (Margalit & Walzer 2009, 21)

As we can see, states are defined as nations and as state-like political bodies and as people, and the wars they are engaged in fall within the purview of just war theory. The mere fact that Hamas has been labeled a terrorist organization by Israel does not give Israel a license to ignore the moral principles of just war theory; just because Hamas thinks Israel does not have the right to exist or to be considered a legitimate state at all, does not give them a license to randomly kill Israeli civilians without a proper declaration of war.

As the authors discuss the 2009 Israeli intervention in Gaza that killed close to one thousand Palestinian civilians, additional difficulties in definition come into play. For example, "the crucial means for limiting the scope of warfare is to draw a sharp line between combatants and noncombatants. This is the only morally relevant distinction that all those involved in a war can agree on" (Ibid.). But, lo and behold, this seemingly simple distinction is fraught with ambiguities: is the only combatant a soldier, or can someone who is providing a safe haven for a soldier be a combatant too? What about those pretending to be noncombatants but who are indeed participating in one form or another in the combat, thus providing undue advantages to one side over the other? Can civilians, then, be a legitimate target? Can they ever be legitimately assassinated by (legitimate state) soldiers? "The presumption of just war theory is that all the combatants believe that their country is fighting a just war" (Ibid.). Margalit and Walzer explain that this is a reasonable presumption, given the kind of education or indoctrination soldiers receive from their community before they even enter war-like situations. Given this, the authors are careful to suggest that perhaps both sides in most wars fight objectively *unjust* wars, but that they *subjectively* believe "that justice is on their side" (Ibid.).

As you can tell from this brief review of the Israeli-Palestinian conflict, it is almost impossible to dissect with any certainty the moral superiority of one side over the other. Both sides appeal to their gods and their sacred texts, the Bible and the Koran; both sides selectively recall their histories and their original claims to the holy land; and both sides accuse one another of terrorist acts of violence. Searching for moral equivalence is futile; the prospect of finding a moral solution is untenable. What remains true for observers of this conflict and unfortunately many others like them, are the complex and contradictory narratives and images that represent them. The images, as we by now realize, do not tell the *whole* or the *true* story; they can only gesture towards this or that aspect of the story. They promise that once we are more informed about the situation and its underlying conditions, we might have a less cavalier or simple-minded judgment about the war that these images represent.

THE POWER OF IMAGES, THE IMAGES
OF POWER: CENSORSHIP

As we argued in our *Political Blind Spots* (2006), the idea that there is a *universal language of art* lends itself to both the fruitful communication across linguistic and cultural boundaries—having symbols and images that can be *read* by anyone anywhere—and to the potential manipulation by propaganda. We recalled there how the Nazis, upon the conquest of Austria, raided the Social and Economic Museum in order to confiscate, and eventually make use of, its treasure-trove of the International System Of TYpographic Picture Education (ISOTYPE). The Nazi propaganda machine was so effective that it was able to garner the support of its own population and inflame the hatred of the Jews, for example, in many other European countries (e.g., Goldhagen 1996). But we would be remiss if we were to confine our discussion of the power of propaganda—spreading a particular doctrine or disseminating an ideology or set of ideals—to fascist regimes of World War II. As we explained with comparative images, the visual framing of democracy was identical in many instances to that of fascism, similar *values* were highlighted by both ideological extremes, and similar *emotional appeals* could be easily detected in the actual posters that were produced between the two world wars (Sassower & Cicotello 2006, ch. 2).

What renders propaganda effective is the way in which it controls information and distills a set of ideas into an easily accessible set of images or phrases ("I Want You for U.S. Army" or "Be All You Can Be"). The control is not limited to the selection process of an image or a phrase, but also entails a repression of images and phrases which contradict or undermine the official doctrinaire message from being *clearly* heard across airwaves or television sets. Any ambiguity, any equivocation may be deemed dangerous and even undermining national security. It is in this sense that censorship is quite similar to and in many cases works hand in hand with the goals of propaganda. Controlling bodies can be political, military, or even entertainment institutions. As the *Encyclopedia Britannica* suggests about censorship, "From the point of view of its moral significance the censorship was the Roman manifestation of that state control of conduct which was a not unusual feature of ancient society." The practice of censorship is ancient and has not lost its appeal for the authorities. If you are worried about your position and the legitimacy of your authority, the best way to ensure obedience and support is to forbid criticism or disagreement. Any idea or image that could be construed as *controversial*—outside the official agenda—would immediately provoke debate or possibly dissent. Where Hitler had his views of "degenerate art"—artworks that were "un-German" in their distorted abstract form and emotional expressionism—contemporary political leaders frown on artworks or images that are deemed *unpatriotic*—depictions of American soldiers as imperialists with Swastika insignia or as torturers.

As we have mentioned earlier, there might be good reasons to *censor*, to suppress what is considered morally or otherwise unacceptable. It is not merely to ensure what LeShan explained in terms of social cohesion and the loyalty one feels for one's community, but also in order to protect certain values shared by a community. We have laws that forbid murder, robbery, or rape; we have institutions—courts, police forces, military defenses—that protect us from each other and the rest of the world. We may change our minds about what values or ideals we wish to herald and protect—from human rights and civil liberties, the right to own guns and have free speech, all the way to abortion rights and same-sex marriages. But in all of these cases, we make it clear that it is the public at large that is involved in and eventually controls the shift in ideology and the means by which this ideology should be realized. The role of censorship, then, has always been suspect in a democracy. In fact, one of the symbols of the radical difference between the United States and the Soviet Union during the Cold War (1945–1991) was our complete freedom of expression and their absolute state of oppression. Yet, the role of censorship, as a means to protect greater ends, remains open-ended itself: under what conditions is it justified? Under what specific circumstances would we all welcome its imposition? For example, would it be in the best national interest *not* to divulge our radar capabilities and satellite defense technology? Wouldn't it be foolish to let everyone know how to produce an atomic bomb? Certainly there are situations when censorship is welcomed and even necessary.

The recent controversies regarding war images associated with but not limited to the ongoing Iraq War have to do with two unrelated issues: torture and death. The torture is of our presumed enemies, and the death is about our warriors. The torture took place in the Abu-Ghraib prison as well as in the Guantanamo Bay military base along with other secret prisons. The death of our soldiers has been primarily from the Iraqi front but also from Afghanistan. When newspapers reported on the debates regarding the publication of "death images," or more precisely images of flag-draped coffins being shipped back to America, set on airport tarmacs or unloaded from cargo-planes, they had two views in mind. On the one hand we had to be sensitive to the families' privacy and also ensure that these images were not politicized. The respect accorded a fallen soldier and the mourning family and friends should be sacred, and should never be compromised for public consumption or political purposes. As such, images shouldn't be widely spread in the media; a moment of silence, a prayer, and private viewing is all that need accompany a soldier's final journey home.

On the other hand, we should not sanitize the casualties of war, and make sure that the public is aware of how costly it is. Soldiers die in the line of duty defending a policy driven by Washington; soldiers sacrifice their lives in order for us to remain secure within our borders; and as such, their sacrifice should be part of the equation of war: is it worth the price? Is the price too high? The minute a soldier puts on a uniform, he or she becomes national property, as military manuals emphasize, accountable to the Commander in Chief and to his lieutenants. Soldiers—however different from us—represent us all, and as such their conduct in war, as Walzer reminds us, must express our moral principles and always be objectively justifiable. This is not a personal war, but a national war that the public supports and has the power to stop. The display of flag-draped coffins, then, is part of the public debate and must never be censored. Along these lines there is also an argument about freedom of expression, our First Amendment to the Constitution, that allows us to display any image we wish so long as it does not *directly* cause harm (in the form of incitement to rioting, for example, or calling "fire" in a crowded hall when no fire is in sight). If we cannot print images of the dead (already debated during and after the Civil War), what else can we not print? This is a logical slippery slope we must avoid! (Seelye 2009, 16).

Arguments can also be presented in a different way. One could focus exclusively on First Amendment rights (of free speech) and thereby trump any attempt of censorship whatsoever. This view was challenged by Justice Potter Stewart in 1971 with this question: "if a disclosure of sensitive information in war time would result in the sentencing to death of a hundred young men whose only offense had been that they have been 19 years old and had low draft numbers?" The lawyer who argued for public disclosure responded: "I'm afraid that my inclinations of humanity overcome the somewhat more abstract devotion to the First Amendment." You see, the theory is applied, the abstract principles must be tested against reality: in order to save the lives of soldiers we must overlook the fine principle of free speech. Of course, the test is difficult to apply ahead of time, because the *potential* injuries or deaths cannot be ascertained with any kind of certainty. So, how can this argument be sustained? In a 1972 case about congressional immunity, Justice William O. Douglas wrote in his dissenting opinion: "As has been revealed by such exposes as the Pentagon Papers, the Mai Lai massacres, the Gulf of Tonkin 'incident,' and the Bay of Pigs invasion, the government usually suppresses damaging news but highlights favorable news" (Liptak 2009, 1). As we can tell from these legal disputes, the question of censorship is both a legal and moral one as well as a question of policy objectives and military safety. The greatest legal minds of the Supreme Court are not unanimous regarding this issue: they worry about the delicate balance between unbridled free speech and the potential and real harm that can be caused to fighting armies. Democratic demands for openness, a basic entitlement to review government policies and hold political and military leaders accountable to the general public come into stark conflict when national security concerns are the responsibility of government officials.

We can recall the outcry that developed with the publication of torture scenes in Abu-Ghraib: the country was shocked, officers were speechless, and soldiers claimed innocence. The world watched with amazement and was quick to judge our inhumanity, our sense of superiority, and our base cruelty and disrespect of others. Likewise, images of Guantanamo Bay and the treatment of prisoners there have been fodder for world-wide criticism for the arbitrary imprisonment of detainees whose right to a fair trial has been denied. Time will tell how some of these issues get resolved in the next few months and years. Is this really how Americans follow their own laws or international laws? Can American values be protected or damaged by their war conduct and the images that represent their behavior? Trying to find a pragmatic fine line between those refusing to release images that could damage America's posture in the world and those demanding full disclosure has been difficult. At first, President Obama offered to release any and all images under the censor's control. Reversing himself in short order, the president had this to say: "The publication of these photos would not add any additional benefit to our understanding of what was carried out in the past by a small number of individuals. In fact, the most direct consequence of releasing them, I believe, would be to further inflame anti-American opinion and put our troops in greater danger" (Ibid., 4). The standard adopted by the Supreme Court (Justice Stewart writing for the majority), in a case demanding access to classified and unclassified materials under the Freedom of Information Act, is that restraint can only be imposed if the disclosure "will surely result in direct, immediate and irreparable damage to our nation or its people" (Ibid.). If we are to follow this standard, and if we are to interpret Obama's argument, then what seems to be the practical conclusion to all of these debates is that the "burden of proof" (in terms of potential harm) lies with those supporting censorship. As we shall see in the next chapter, state censorship can easily become a self-imposed censorship fueled by sentiments of patriotism.

4

THE PRAGMATIC
PROMISE

THE MORAL DIMENSIONS OF WAR AND TERRORISM

We ended the previous chapter with the proposal regarding the need to maintain a delicate balance between the public's right to know everything about wars and the need to conceal sensitive materials that might cause harm to our troops at war. Whether this balance is set up by the Supreme Court or by the president makes no difference. What matters in every case when this balance is challenged is the way the public accepts or rejects this balance, the way the public responds to what is being done in its name and on its behalf. As citizens we should be involved as much as possible with the affairs of the state, but we end up worrying about our own situation, our family finances, and the health of our extended family. We neither have the time nor the resources to follow the intricacies of legal disputations and what the outcome of these disputations may turn out to be. In short, we rely on experts and politicians we trust to clarify the intricacies of warfare for us. We count on television pundits, political bloggers, and newscasters to deliver the data as objectively as possible; we count on our representatives to be our watchdogs. We have found over the years how difficult it is even for experts to explain what we are up against. One day it is a "war on terrorism" and the next day we are "freedom fighters" liberating the oppressed Iraqi people; one day we are gaining advantage in the world arena by controlling oil fields (Iraq supposedly has the third largest reservoir of oil in the world) and the next day we are defending our positions against the imminent encroachment of Iranian forces. One day we are engaged in the Middle East for the long-run and the next day we are a global "police force" enforcing, as it were, United Nations' resolutions. In short, foreign policy seems confused and is confusing, especially as we move from one administration to the next.

After 9/11 everything changed in the American intellectual and security landscapes: we felt for the first time in centuries a kind of vulnerability reserved for other countries; we experienced a shocking violation of our security and a sense of fear we have associated with so-called third world countries. If Kamikaze fighters seemed "crazy" to us, we could still make sense of their appearance during World War II: they were our *enemies* and their actions were undertaken within the context of a declared war. American civilian airplanes flying into the Twin Towers in broad daylight (with civilian passengers on board) was an unexpected event: we were not at war with these terrorists and did not expect such an attack. Put differently, whatever literature prepared us for *just* or *unjust war* did not cover such an incident. Under these circumstances, it is understandable that a new set of linguistic terms and safety policies would be enacted. But as we have moved into the twenty-first century, the categories used by the Supreme Court in light of the Vietnam War may not hold (mentioned briefly at the end of the previous chapter), as the technologies of war have transformed not only war strategies and tactics but the very notion of what it is to *fight a war*.

When President Bush announced his "war on terror" in the aftermath of 9/11, he in fact ushered a new dawn for warfare and for the discussion of war. The subjects of Walzer's arguments in 1977 became somewhat outdated because his concern with guerilla warfare and terrorist activities were peripheral to his moral argument about conventional wars. As we have seen in the previous chapter, he has reassessed his own theory in light of contemporary conflicts, such as the Israeli-Palestinian one, where claims of terrorism dominate the discourse and as such raise questions about the application of just and unjust *war* theory; should it now be called *just* and *unjust terrorist theory*? While this question is being asked, more detailed accounts of the differences between conventional warfare and terrorist acts should be given as well. What is the difference between them, if they both result in death? The philosopher Simon Keller, for one, suggests that "terrorism is not, in all its forms, something that ought to be opposed," since there are those occasions with "sufficient causes" where "terrorism can be justified—justified for much the same reasons that all-out war can be justified." When this happens, "there are too many hazards associated with real-world judgments about who is and who is not a terrorist" (Keller 2005, 67). For some terrorism is about the progress and level of technologies that are being used and abused against certain groups (McReynolds 2005), while for others it is a semantic matter wherein "one man's terrorist is another man's heroic martyr" (Fiala 2005, 100). Others associate terrorism with forms of physical violence and assess their appropriateness in terms of how much violence is ever justified (Govier 2005), and there are numerous others, finally, who attempt to extend Walzer's original text (and the categories he used) to the contemporary context (Besser-Jones 2005 and Kessler 2005). Finally, there are those who claim that America's own foreign policies are "terrorist" in more than one sense, thereby turning the focus on our state-sanctioned conduct rather than the conduct of our "enemies" (Gareau 2004).

As can be seen from this brief and sketchy survey, the definitions we use in order to describe the difference between war and terrorism are problematic, and as such don't lend themselves easily to the kind of "black-and-white" moral judgment we'd like to have. Perhaps Philip Heymann is correct in proclaiming that "we have used 'war' metaphorically to indicate any relative massive commitment of attention, energy, and resources to a dangerous problem. Thus we have committed ourselves, in the last half-century, to 'wars' on poverty, crime, and drugs" (Heymann 2003, 20). This is an excellent point, because it illustrates the *metaphorical* and therefore symbolic character of wars and why we have been so concerned with war images and their impact on public policies. Our own concern with images and how to read them can provide some tools for those engaged in developing strategic approaches to encounter terrorism in a fashion that depends on international cooperation and the promotion of civil liberties. Before we offer some of our own suggestions of how the reading of war images can also contribute a practical approach to promoting peace rather than perpetuating wars, we'd like to follow closely the comments of two legal theorists who build on Walzer's theory for the international context.

What Walzer offered in the wake of the Vietnam War (since he remains a benchmark for most war theorists) is what George Fletcher and Jens David Ohlin offer in their *Defending Humanity* (2008) in the wake of the wars in Afghanistan and Iraq: a coherent and philosophically grounded analysis and a set of prescriptions of how we should handle international affairs. Though Walzer's concern was to provide a moral argument while Fletcher and Ohlin's concern is to provide a legal framework, both sets of authors acknowledge that arguing from practical prudence or exigency alone is not enough (Ibid., xvi). What is required is a thoughtful and critical grounding that can then be used to confront other situations and engage other countries in an appropriate manner. The rhetoric of the media and politicians seems misguided once we take a more careful look at the conditions under which wars are declared and under which they are executed. This is true not only in cases where politicians want to mislead the public, but also in cases where they only try to over-simplify their deliberations. The media pundits are then left with their own overly simplified—accessible—description or analysis of the situation, and in doing so exacerbate the process of misleading or not fully explaining the conditions of war. Likewise, one cannot justify a declaration of war by simply relying on a UN Article (passed by the Security Council, for example), since the circumstances vary in each case. The variance requires a level of sophistication that typically goes beyond the politicians' inclination to detail their deliberations and the media's reporting interests. When the media fails to provide critical thinking and reflection, we may have to look for others to provide a useful conceptual framework. This kind of framework is brilliantly offered by Fletcher and Ohlin, perhaps because they are not only academics but also legal scholars, trained in the art of subtle disputation and interpretation.

The novel features identified by the authors in their analysis are: first, they "draw on the analogy between self-defense in domestic law and in international law" (Ibid., vii). They were able to identify cases which demonstrate nuances of the law, some dating back to Biblical times, which may be helpful in assessing the international cases that have recently appeared. Second, "to pursue this analogy we pay closer attention to the comparative law of self-defense than is usually done in conventional work on international law" (Ibid., viii). This means that they draw on the French as well as the English interpretations of Article 51 of the UN's Charter "which limits the use of force to situations called self-defense, or legitimate defense" (Ibid.). In this book the basic "unquestioned truth" is that "military action is justified under international law only in two situations. First, the United Nations Security Council can authorize the use of military force to restore collective peace and security. Secondly, military action is legal even in the absence of Security Council authorization, but the United Nations Charter explicitly limits this use of military force to self-defense" (Ibid., 3). The crux of the matter, then, is how one defines self-defense and whether or not the definition being used can be justified in a court of law.

Using a variety of international cases in which self-defense claims have been made, the authors painstakingly differentiate each case and its set of conditions from the others, so as to illustrate how complex the notion of self-defense in fact is, and how often it is carelessly or inappropriately invoked in legal terms. Domestic cases of self-defense can be informative for the international community if and only if some basic assumptions are agreed upon. First, "when nations act *as a collective group,* certain standards apply, and we hold states responsible when they fail to live up to them. When soldiers act *as individuals,* criminal law applies, and we put them on trial when they break the law" (Ibid., 11). Secondly, "international law *treats* nations as moral and rational agents, regardless of the degree to which they actually approximate this ideal" (Ibid.). And thirdly, "international law grants legal *personality* to nation-states and treats them as the kind of entities that have moral and legal interests, rights, and responsibilities. They can be held accountable for their actions just like human beings" (Ibid.). These assumptions help make the case for comparing the domestic and international legal frameworks, and because these assumptions are not simply legal axioms but philosophically loaded concepts, the authors take the time to refer to Kant, Rawls, and Walzer as philosophers whose own definitions and arguments are worthy of reconsideration. The ability to weave old philosophical principles and ideas into the fabric of contemporary conflicts shines through the discussions of Fletcher and Ohlin.

Their references are not limited to philosophers and legal scholars. They regularly refer to the Bible as a source for ancient religious thinking and moral behavior that were assembled into a set of rules and laws. They cite Leviticus 19:16, "Do not stand idly by while your neighbor bleeds" (Ibid., 49), as the duty to rescue those under duress; they cite a third-party duty to intervene in cases of self-defense under French law (Ibid., 44); and they also explain the domestic-international axis of legal interpretation (Ibid., 81) as it relates to cases of self-defense. From these and other sources they conclude with some of the general distinctions about the four models of self-defense. The first is related to punishment as "just desert" (Ibid., 55), the second to "excuse," insofar as it is not a direct punishment of wrongdoing but as an Old English legal appreciation of "the predicament of the trapped defender" (Ibid., 58), the third is "justified defense of autonomy," vindicating the fundamental right of each person to her or his autonomy (Ibid., 59), and the fourth is the defense of society so that one's actions are understood in terms of furthering the public good or the well-being of society as a whole (Ibid., 60–61). These four models help delineate the multiple principles that are routinely invoked in domestic court cases, and whose distinctions can shed light on the confusion faced by international criminal courts when addressing national or individual politicians' violations of the United Nations' Charter.

In general, the Western world has prided itself on being concerned with humanitarian aid and intervention on behalf of suffering people around the globe. In some ways, this concern has identified the Western world as *more progressive* than the rest of the world, claiming a certain moral high-ground. The authors remind us that we "are hardly acting in collective self-defense. . . . Rather, the pertinent issue is whether the humanitarian crisis is legally sufficient to justify a violation of another state's territorial integrity on the basis of defense of others" (Ibid., 69). Our moral inclination is to condone any and every humanitarian act, yet we may fail to see that our sanction might be *morally justifiable* but *legally questionable*. Our sanction, then, would violate our deeply held political and legal views and doctrines that respect national autonomy. This legal caveat becomes even more complex when we deal with an international arena in which cultures and their languages may not have the same or even similar concepts, such as rights, a "highly individualistic notion foreign to the Japanese legal system" (Ibid., 75). The use of domestic legal systems to enlighten the international community may work on one level of extrapolation; but when different countries cannot even agree on the definitions of the basic concepts or do not have words to describe them as part of their lexicon, then overall confusion might ensue. This confusion, in turn, necessitates a secondary level of interpretation that itself may add confusion rather than clarification. The four models of domestic self-defense are problematic at the domestic legal level, and once applied to the international community would remain as problematic; they can still be helpful guides for teasing out the relevant facts and circumstances in each case (Ibid., 82–84).

According to Fletcher and Ohlin, there are six elements of legitimate defense: "three bearing on the nature of the attack and three on the requirements for permissible defense" (Ibid., 86). According to Fletcher and Ohlin, the attack must be overt, unlawful, and imminent, while the defense must be necessary, proportional, and knowing or intentional in response to the attack (Ibid., 86–87). For the attack to be overt, "there must be an event that the whole world can see to justify the use of force" (Ibid., 89). For the attack to be unlawful, we must appreciate that "justified actions are not unlawful; excused actions are" (Ibid.). For the attack to be imminent, "legitimate self-defense must be neither too soon nor too late" (Ibid., 90). For the defense to be necessary, "the criterion of necessity makes sense when we are talking about preventing a current attack or frustrating the commission of crimes, but not when the purpose is preventing or deterring successive attacks" (Ibid., 95). For the defense to be proportional, what is required is "a balancing of competing interests: the interests of the defender and those of the aggressor" (Ibid., 96). In this context the authors refer to tort cases to explain the notion and practical implications of proportionality (Ibid., 100–102). The sixth element of intentional or knowing response has to do with an understanding of the response as "a privilege that can be properly exercised only by people who know the relevant facts," so as to eliminate pretexts for unjustified attacks (Ibid., 105).

Invariably the authors return to questions of humanitarian intervention, perhaps because the legal systems we have constructed after World War II were predicated on wholesale human rights violations and genocide. Once Nazi doctors, for example, were brought to trial, it was crucial to establish a legitimate tribunal that had the authority to hear their cases and punish them. So, cases of "putative self-defense" or "reasonable mistake of fact as an excuse" must be reconsidered on the international level, with "actors" (states) that are presumed to be like individuals in terms of their rights and duties, their moral responsibilities and protections. No matter how clear the authors are in providing four models of self-defense or six elements of justified self-defense, they are patently aware of the difficulties that still prevail in trying to ascertain which of the models or elements are present in specific cases. Our perceptions differ because we have different perspectives and different backgrounds and histories. For example, applying a "cost/benefit approach to international disputes" would be extremely complicated and fall short of clearly assigning guilt or innocence in cases of self-defense (Ibid., 166). The collective dimension of national behavior and actions is problematic because "the collective army might be liable for aggression, but nothing about the guilt of individuals follows from this charge" (Ibid., 190), and vice versa, the guilt of one criminal soldier in and of itself does not engender a liability for the whole army or nation.

Perhaps it is fitting after such a close reading of Fletcher and Ohlin's book to summarize their main point by quoting the last sentence of the book, as it summarizes the sense of legitimating that which we hope never to legitimate, namely, the use of force: "the use of legitimate defense is the lawful and justified use of violence, which can prevail in the face of a nation's worst nightmare: an attack from beyond its horizon, or even from within" (Ibid., 218).

FABRICATED WAR IMAGES AS PRAGMATIC POLITICS

The dilemma faced by politicians, rather than by scholars, is not so much how and under what conditions to use *legitimate* defense, but how to legitimize it to the general public. We never know all the relevant facts because in cases of national security they are classified state secrets and should be protected from public disclosure. So, the public tends to give its leaders the benefit of the doubt, believe that indeed government agencies and political leaders fulfill their fiduciary responsibility and represent the will of the people and its best interests. Otherwise, the government could not properly function in a democracy. This is not a patronizing posture claiming that the government knows best or that the public is too ignorant to participate in the decision-making process. Instead, this is a practical and informed decision by the public to delegate its authority, its "sovereign rights," as war theorists realize, to political leaders.

Some might worry that even in a democracy censorship may turn into self-censorship. Self-censorship can be understood psychologically, where internalizing norms and taboos eventually makes us feel guilty about certain actions we take (stealing, cheating, and the like). It can also be understood socially, where peer pressure forces people to conform to social norms that they would otherwise not agree with (making racist or sexist or anti-Semitic comments, for example). Similarly, self-censorship can be understood politically, where military leaders confide in political leaders and thereby exclude the public from the decision-making process (deciding, for example, to declare war). Self-censorship is a dangerous mind-set that should be discouraged. We should always feel free to ask the most awkward questions (as we do when we confront presidents and senators and congress-members about their financial and amorous affairs), and the most annoying questions (as we do when we challenge a decision retroactively and demand to know the reasons for making it). No question should ever remain unanswered, even when national security considerations are at stake. On the contrary, when national security is at stake more questions need to be asked. If citizens cannot ask them, then their representatives must, and if they fail to do so, lawyers and judges should.

As we tried to demonstrate throughout this book, our concerns with politics are related to the question of how political positions and decisions are being *fabricated*: how they are constructed and presented. So, for example, when it was pointed out that certain images were *staged* (including images not reproduced in this book, such as the iconic battlefield photograph depicting the raising of the flag on Iwo Jima), our intent was not to focus on the *fabrication* itself, but rather to highlight the fact that such a fabrication took place at all. This proves the point that the power of images is so immense that image makers and public relations experts make an effort to *perfectly stage the ultimate symbol* of heroism, patriotism, or whatever else they thought was worthy for public consumption back home. Images are enormously powerful and are an influential tool of communication that needs to be handled carefully, since they can be manipulated or misread. For instance, recall General Colin Powell presenting the American reasons to launch a war against Iraq at the UN, asking for its sanction (as Fletcher and Ohlin argue). In order to amplify his points, enlarged photographs were shown, presumably of mobile rocket launchers that were a threat to world peace (the infamous weapons of mass destruction). Why the photos? Why not stick with statistical analysis and intelligence reports or data collected by the UN inspectors? The images could convince where words would fail; the photos could be *read universally*, whereas English words would have to be translated into numerous other languages and perhaps something would be lost in translation. The response was immediate, and the UN sanctioned the American invasion. During the Cuban Missile Crisis in 1962, enlarged aerial photographs were also presented to the UN delegates to support the American claim that the Soviet Union was amassing nuclear rockets close enough to U.S. soil to be a real and immediate threat.

The use of images for political purposes is not limited, of course, to warfare. One photograph of Senator Gary Hart of Colorado on a boat with a young woman that was not his wife derailed his presidential candidacy. One television image of an empty House of Representatives in session with only two out of four hundred thirty five members tells volumes about the lack of dedication of politicians and their disrespect towards their constituents. One image on a button or bumper-sticker can affect how we think about political issues, from abortion to gay marriages, from nuclear disarmament to sustainability. But unlike a campaign that ends abruptly or an embarrassing image that hurts someone's feelings, the stakes are much higher in the case of war. The Gary Harts of this country usually end up having lucrative alternative careers, while soldiers sent to an unnecessary battle may end up dead.

As we illustrated in chapter 2, whether a single image or a cluster of images, every one of them can become iconic, a powerful symbol for an idea or situation, or can encapsulate an entire set of emotions and reactions. "The Kiss" of World War II (p. 32) is quite different from many kisses exchanged by returning soldiers and their loved ones. We all have witnessed in the past few years soldiers returning from Iraq and Afghanistan and being greeted at airports and military bases. Why have their kisses not captured our imagination as much as the canonic one of World War II? Are they any less meaningful? Perhaps "The Kiss" symbolized the victory of the allied forces in World War II and the end of that war, while all the contemporary *kisses* remind the soldiers and their loved ones that yet another tour of duty is possible, that the wars are not over, and that soldiers' return is not final. You could review the images in chapter 2 and probably come up with numerous contemporary parallels. The same

questions can be asked which would result in several different answers (depending on the specific context and circumstances of the
situation). A similar analysis could be made of the idyllic image of
the girl in the field of flowers (in the cluster of the Afghanistan War
images): one must know what kind of flowers these are and that
opium is produced from them; one must know the history of the
opium trade in this region; one must know how this trade has funded
warlords in the area; one must know that some of these warlords are
involved in terrorist activities; and one must know about the recent
political situation in Afghanistan and the American involvement
there since 9/11. From innocence and playfulness we quickly shift to
the global war on terrorism, and from one image a whole tale can be
spun. What tale would others spin? Is there a tale that is more *real* or
true? Whose perspective should dominate public discourse? And to
what extent are politicians themselves caught up in accepting tales
spun by others (experts, spies, foreign correspondents)?

So when we allude to *pragmatic politics* we don't mean that which
works or makes sense at the moment. Instead, we suggest following the insistence of American Pragmatists that meaning and truth
depend on the circumstances under which they are examined, and
that they are conventional in the sense that we all agree that something is true or has meaning. As such, political discourse differs
from religious or moral discourse: while the former is more apt to be
flexible in its wording and definitions, meaning, and interpretation,
the latter two are prone to have a set of principles and foundations
which are solid and permanent. If we find killing to be wrong from
a Biblical and a moral perspective (an absolute prohibition), there
may be some wiggle room for it in political and legal discourses
(self-defense or warfare or other circumstances). The flexibility allowed by political discourse is not a license to lie or manipulate or
distort reality. Rather, it is an invitation to be more vigilant about
critically examining the conditions under which a meaning changes
(sacrificing one's life for a cause), a definition is reworded (terrorism), or a policy is adapted (declaration of war). If we are aware that
political discourse is inherently more problematic, we should not respond with cynicism or a yawn, but rather become actively engaged

is deconstructing the symbols and metaphors, learning more about the context of the debate, and making sure that displayed images *fit* whatever ideological claims are being made. This is not to say that we must agree or disagree with the *images* or the *ideology,* but rather that we should ask interesting and provocative questions about the images, the ideologies, and their relationships before we accept or reject any of them.

As discussed elsewhere (Sassower 1997), there is also a psycho-social dimension to this view of images and wars and knowledge in general. We swiftly move from a level of *ambiguity,* where scientific data, or in our case data about a war, are so ambiguous that one is not likely to end up with knowledge that is certain or with a conclusion to an experiment or war report that is clear-cut. This inherent ambiguity leads inevitably to a level of *anxiety,* where cultural responses are confused and confusing, and where individual feelings are fraught with anxiety about what should be known and what can be known. Ambiguity necessarily leads to anxiety, and in turn this social anxiety permeates every individual psyche. This psycho-social process leads to a level of *anguish,* where one feels that there is no way to ever get clarity about whatever set of data one is interested in figuring out: in our case, should we be in this war? Should we have entered it to begin with? Whom should we trust with the presentation of data, the CIA, the military, the national security representatives, the Department of Defense, the Secretary of State, the president? When this deep level of distrust is shared by a great number of people, there is a sense of anguish that undermines the kind of patriotism or heroism we commonly associate with protecting our nation and waging war on our enemies. So, we believe it is necessary to mention this psycho-social process in passing to ensure that we don't deal exclusively with political or ethical abstractions.

PEDAGOGY OF CRITICAL AESTHETIC ENGAGEMENT

We have given numerous examples of the main arguments of this book: images are powerful, powerful images can sway and even determine public opinion, images can have multiple interpretations, images can be staged or fabricated, fabrication and staging of images can falsify facts and their presentation, political agendas can be read off images even when they may not appear to be overtly political in nature, war images have a particular emotive impact on viewers, and the arguments for and against wars, for example, are magnified and clearly distilled when reviewing war images.

In light of this, then, we'd like to conclude this book with a set of recommendations. They are general but also personal insofar as they place the responsibility of reading war images on the spectator and not the producer or disseminator of these images. The question is: what can *you* do about it, rather than what do *they* have to do to change their image presentation? We assume that individuals remain powerless to change political institutions in general, but that they always have the power to challenge and criticize, ask questions and demand answers. This personal (and eventually communal) process may bring about a change: provoking the national mind-set to be rethought or maybe even transformed. Therefore, we recommend that images should be contextualized as much as possible within their own frames of references and also outside of them (see our analysis of the benefits and limitations of modernist and postmodernist interpretations). Likewise, images must be contrasted with other images in order to create a certain perceptual and cognitive tension: should I believe what I see? Should I look elsewhere for more clues to solve this visual puzzle (in foreign media, in more websites)? Moreover, we recommend reading war images the way one would read complex books and essays, slowly, methodically, and critically, so that we might not miss an important element or hint that reveals the nature of the debate. As we argued throughout the book, images are not as transparent as they may seem at first. And finally, we insist that the promise of a universal visual language may not be attainable at all, due to the bounty of cultural differences that persist in the face of globalization. For example, what is torture to us may be appropriate punishment to others, just as kissing in public is romantic in one culture and deemed pornographic in another. These recommendations are not limited to students in higher education institutions, but should extend to military personnel that already receive training in cross-cultural sensitivity, as well as to the public at large. Late-night hosts could spend a few minutes every night reviewing a war image and providing a set of contrasting interpretations, some serious, some humorous, in order to break down the false perception that an image says it all and is fixed in its meaning. Since we believe that an image is worth a thousand words, these words are hopefully critical, are engaged, and provide a spectrum of interpretative options.

Throughout this book we argue that wars are in fact waged visually and not only on the battlefield. Image warfare is as potent and at times preempts an actual war because the warring sides could be dissuaded from embarking on a war that would bring about mutual disaster. Soldiers feel emboldened when the enemy is portrayed as evil and deserving to die, or safe knowing that their army is strong and well-equipped to fight a war. The public, likewise, can be persuaded that a war is justified given certain images of the enemy, such as the cruelty to its own civilians (as Saddam Hussein was portrayed in the months leading to the invasion of Iraq). Images are time sensitive and so it is important to note when and how they are displayed or distributed for public consumption. If displayed too soon, they can be forgotten by the time a congressional debate takes place; if displayed too late they may lose their effectiveness; if displayed too often, the public may become disinterested; if displayed not often enough, the public may forget what the issue was all about.

If war images are potent elements in waging wars and if their display is time sensitive, we should also be concerned with their temporary value. Unlike some canonical images that transcend a particular war and ensure our sense of patriotism (raising of the American flag in battle or a romantic reunion of a soldier with loved ones), most war images are more limited in their scope of appeal: they make a point about an issue (torture), a consequence (nuclear attack), or a period (Civil War). The temporality of war images also depends, as we tried to illustrate, on the medium that carries them to public view: paintings, drawings, photographs, films, videos, cell-phone snap-shots, satellite images, and many others. The medium of production, distribution, and consumption depends on the progress of visual technologies. These technologies, as was argued in chapter 3 in relation to terrorism, change not only the medium itself but also the nature of the presentation. Just as new technologies have blurred the difference between war and terrorism (where weaponry and tactics are more easily attainable by rogue groups), so do new visual technologies contribute to blurring the difference between war and peace. In other words, we can present a conflict as mild or monumental, benign or devastating with the power of the camera, with a click of a finger. We can overwhelm or underwhelm our viewers with a single shot. And as technologies change, they transform the visual vocabulary we have available to us to judge a war-like situation and its severity.

Because of the continuous change in technologies of perception, our recommendations for critical visual assessments become even more urgent. When the Internet usurps all other forms of data collection and communication, we ought to be alert to the dangers and opportunities that come with this usurpation. When YouTube and Facebook become powerful means of information dissemination, because of their instant transmission—their virtual immediacy—we must learn how to *read* and *interpret* their messages and images as if they were in the print media: what legitimacy should they be granted? What credibility do they deserve? What filters do they go through, if any? Are they censored in any sense of the term? Internet websites are here to stay, and *Wikipedia* is more useful and accessible than the *Encyclopedia Britannica*, regardless of the objections of some academics and scholars who worry about accuracy and reliability. The information hierarchies of yesteryear are crumbling, and a new intellectual world order is upon us: we can engage it critically and enjoy its fruits rather than resort to an old-fashioned model that is more cumbersome and less user-friendly. New information and visual technologies should be liberating (with a democratic appeal) and as such should be inviting to all of us to participate more regularly in critically assessing their effectiveness and reliability. We can use the Internet to challenge the authorities and their dissemination of information and images rather than retreat to mindless entertainment provided by athletic events and music concerts. The Internet as a resource can be a treasure-trove worthy of careful engagement with enlightening results. This is not a promotion of the Internet because of its immediacy of data transmission. Rather, this medium simply illustrates the expansion of image resources and their access to wider audiences. The complexity and gravity of reading war images demands our dedication to critically examine all media sources whatever their next technological phase may be.

BIBLIOGRAPHY

Aristophanes. "Lysistrata" in *Four Comedies*. Translated by D. Fitts. New York: Harcourt, Brace & World, Inc., [412 BCE] 1957.

Balken, Debra Bricker. *Debating American Modernism: Stieglitz, Duchamp, and the New York Avant-Garde*. New York: American Federation of Arts, 2003.

Barzun, Jacques. *The Use and Abuse of Art*. Princeton and London: Princeton University Press, 1974.

Besser-Jones, Lorraine. "Just War Theory: Legitimate Authority, and the 'War' on Terror," in *Philosophy 9/11: Thinking about the War on Terrorism*, edited by Timothy Shanahan. Chicago and LaSalle, IL: Open Court, 2005, pp. 129–48.

Bogard, Michele H. *Artists, Advertising, and the Borders of Art*. University of Chicago Press, 1995.

Brennen, Bonnie, and Hanno Hardt, eds. *Picturing the Past: Media, History, and Photography*. Urbana: University of Illinois Press, 1999.

Clausewitz, Carl von. *On War*. Translated by Michael Howard and Peter Paret. New York: Oxford University Press, [1832–1834] 1976.

——. *On War*. Translated by M. Howard and P. Paret. Oxford: Oxford University Press, [1832] 2007.

——. *Principles of War*. Translated by H. W. Gatzke. Mineola, NY: Dover Publications, [1832–1837] 2003.

Danto, Arthur. "Art after the End of Art," in *Embodied Meanings: Critical Essays and Aesthetic Meditations*. New York: Farrar Straus Giroux, 1994, pp. 321–33.

Faust, Drew Gilpin. *This Republic of Suffering: Death and the American Civil War*. New York: Alfred A. Knopf, 2008.

Fiala, Andrew. "Defusing Fear: A Critical Response to the War on Terrorism," in *Philosophy 9/11: Thinking about the War on Terrorism*, edited by Timothy Shanahan. Chicago and LaSalle, IL: Open Court, 2005, pp. 93–106.

Fletcher, George P., and Jens David Ohlin. *Defending Humanity: When Force Is Justified and Why*. Oxford: Oxford University Press, 2008.

Fry, Roger. *Reflections on British Painting*. London: Ayer Co. Publishers, 1934.

Galbraith, Peter W. *Unintended Consequences: How War in Iraq Strengthened America's Enemies*. New York, Simon & Schuster, 2008.

Gareau, Frederick H. *State Terrorism and the United States: From Counterinsurgency to the War on Terrorism*. Atlanta: Clarity Press, 2004.

Goldhagen, Daniel Jonah. *Hitler's Willing Executioners: Ordinary Germans and the Holocaust*. New York: Alfred A. Knopf, 1996.

Gombrich, E. H. *Art and Illusion: A Study in the Psychology of Pictorial Representation*. Princeton, NJ: Princeton University Press, 1960.

Govier, Trudy. "Physical Violence in Political Conflicts: Grounds for a Strong Presumption against Violence," in *Philosophy 9/11: Thinking about the War on Terrorism*, edited by Timothy Shanahan. Chicago and LaSalle, IL: Open Court, 2005, pp. 107–26.

Greenberg, Clement. *Art and Culture: Critical Essays*. Boston: Beacon Press, 1961.

Haass, Richard N. *War of Necessity, War of Choice: A Memoir of Two Iraq Wars*. New York: Simon & Schuster, 2009.

Hanson, Norwood Russell. *Patterns of Discovery*. London and New York: Cambridge University Press, [1958] 1965.

Heymann, Philip B. *Terrorism, Freedom, and Security: Winning without War*. Cambridge and London: The MIT Press, 2003.

Hoesterey, Ingeborg, ed. *Zeitgeist in Babel: The Postmodernist Controversy*. Bloomington: Indiana University Press, 1991.

Kant, Immanuel. "To Perpetual Peace: A Philosophical Sketch," in *Perpetual Peace and Other Essays on Politics, History, and Morals*. Translated by T. Humphrey. Indianapolis: Hackett Publishing Co., [1795] 1983.

Keller, Simon. "On What Is the War on Terror," in *Philosophy 9/11: Thinking about the War on Terrorism*, edited by Timothy Shanahan. Chicago and LaSalle, IL: Open Court, 2005, pp. 53-68.

——. "Moral Justification for Violent Responses to Terrorism," in *Philosophy 9/11: Thinking about the War on Terrorism*, edited by Timothy Shanahan. Chicago and LaSalle, IL: Open Court, 2005, pp. 149–70.

Kessler, Brett, "Moral Justification for Violent Responses to Terrorism," in *Philosophy 9/11: Thinking*, edited by Timothy Shanahan. Chicago and LaSalle, IL: Open Court, 2005, pp. 149–70.

Kolb, Robert. "Just War." *International Review of the Red Cross* 320 (1997): 553–62.

LeShan, Lawrence. *The Psychology of War: Comprehending Its Mystique and Its Madness.* New York: Helios Press, [1992] 2002.

Liptak, Adam. "Images, the Law and War," *The New York Times*, Sunday, May 17, 2009, pp. 1, 4.

Lyotard, Jean-Francois. *The Postmodern Condition: A Report on Knowledge.* Translated by G. Bennington and B. Massumi. Minneapolis: University of Minnesota Press, [1979] 1984.

Lyotard, Jean-François and Jean-Loup Thebaud. *Just Gaming.* Translated by Wlad Godzich. Minneapolis: University of Minnesota Press, [1979] 1985.

——. *Heidegger and "The Jews."* Translated by A. Michel and M. S. Roberts. Minneapolis: University of Minnesota Press, [1988] 1990.

——. *The Inhuman: Reflections on Time.* Translated by G. Bennington and R. Bowlby. Stanford, CA: Stanford University Press, [1988] 1991.

Machiavelli, Niccolo. *The Art of War.* Translated by E. Farneworth and revised by N. Wood. Cambridge, MA: Da Capo Press, [1521] 1965.

Margalit, Avishai, and Michael Walzer. "Israel: Civilians & Combatants." *The New York Review of Books* LVI:8 (2009): 21–22.

Mays, Dorothy A. *Women in Early America: Struggle, Survival, and Freedom in a New World.* Santa Barbara, CA: ABC-CLIO, 2004.

McReynolds, Phillip. "Terrorism as a Technological Concept: How Low versus High Technology Defines Terrorism and Dictates Our Responses," in *Philosophy 9/11: Thinking about the War on Terrorism*, edited by Timothy Shanahan. Chicago and LaSalle, IL: Open Court, 2005, pp. 69–89.

Moseley, Alexander. "Just War," in *The Internet Encyclopedia of Philosophy*, 2005.

Neurath, Otto. *Empiricism and Sociology.* Edited by Marie Neurath and Robert S. Cohen. Dodrecht and Boston: Reidel (especially ch. 7), 1973.

Nietzsche, Friedrich. *Human, All Too Human*, in *A Nietzsche Reader*, translated by R. J. Hollinger. New York: Penguin Books, [1878] 1977.

Paxton, Robert O. *The Anatomy of Fascism.* New York: Vintage, 2005.

Popper, Karl. *Conjectures and Refutations: The Growth of Scientific Knowledge*. New York: Harper & Row, 1963.

Sassower, Raphael. *Technoscientific Angst: Ethics and Responsibility*. Minneapolis and London: University of Minnesota Press, 1997.

Sassower, Raphael, and Louis Cicotello. *The Golden Avant-Garde*. Charlottesville: University of Virginia Press, 2000.

——. *Political Blind Spots: Reading the Ideology of Images*. Lanham, MD: Lexington Books, 2006.

Seelye, Katherine Q. "Coffins' Arrival from War Becomes an Issue Again as Photo Ban Is Reviewed," *The New York Times*, Sunday, February 22, 2009, p. 16.

Smith, Adam. *An Inquiry into the Nature and Causes of the Wealth of Nations*. Edited by E. Cannan. New York: The Modern Library, [1776] 1937.

Sun Tzu. *The Art of War*. Translated by L. Giles. Mineola, NY: Dover Publications, [500 BCE] 2002.

Walzer, Michael. *Just and Unjust Wars: A Moral Argument with Historical Illustrations*. New York: Basic Books, 1977.

White, Matt. *Cameras on the Battlefield: Photos of War*. Kent, OH: Capstone Press, 2002.

Wittgenstein, Ludwig. *Tractatus Logico-Philosophicus*. London: Routledge & Kegan Paul, [1922] 1958.

——. *Philosophical Investigations*. Translated by G.E.M. Anscombe, New York: Macmillan, 1958.

INDEX

Abu-Ghraib, 89–90

Adams, Eddie, 63

aesthetics: modernist, xiii, 3–9,11–13, 17; postmodernist, xiii, 3–9, 11–12, 14, 18; sublime, 6–9. *See also* Kant

Afghanistan War, 36–37, 42, 55–56, 63–64

Afghan Poppy Field, 36, 64

Agent Orange, 53, 63

Al-Qaeda, 56, 63

American exceptionalism, 50

American pragmatists, 104

Annan, Kofi, 58, 65

Arafat and Annan Meet in Gaza, 40, 65

Arafat, Yasir, 58, 65, 72

Arendt, Hannah, 54

Aristophanes, 76

art: cultural power of, 1–2; death of, 5, 9; degenerate, 88; distribution and consumption of, 2; modern, 4–5; universal language of, ix, 87. *See also* avant-garde; Danto; Greenberg; political-revolutionary; Santa Fe

Atomic Bomb Cloud Over Nagasaki, Japan, 21, 33, 62

avant-garde, 4, 6; art of, 12; cultural role of, ix; and kitsch, 4–5

Barzun, Jacques, 1–2

Black Flags, 30, 62

Blanchard, Kevin, 64

Brady, Mathew, 61

Burial at Sea, 33, 62

Bush administration, 19, 55

Bush, George W., 57, 74, 94

censorship, 88, 101–2

Chemical Defoliant Dispersal, 35, 63

the Christos, 52, 73

Civil War. *See* United States of America Civil War

Code Napolean. *See* Napoleonic Code

Coffins of Iraq War Casualties, 39, 64

Cold War, 51, 88

critical engagement, vii, x–xi, xiv, 45

Cuban Missile Crisis, 103

Dachau Concentration Camp, 32, 52, 62

Danto, Arthur: on death of art, 4–5; 11

David, Jacques Louis, 59, 70–71

Desert Storm, 56, 74

detached engagement, ix–x

Disasters of War: Fatal Consequences of the Bloody War in Spain Against Bonaparte, 26, 60

Douglas, William O., 90

Duchamp, Marcel, 13

Eisenstaedt, Alfred, 62

Encyclopedia Britiannica, 19–20, 108

Enlightenment, 3, 60

exceptionalism. *See* American exceptionalism

Execution of a Viet Cong Prisoner, 35, 63

fabrication of reality. *See* war images

Facebook, 1

Faust, Drew Gilpin, 46

Fighting in the Tora Bora, 37, 63

the Final Solution, 52

Flagg, John Montgomery, 61

Fletcher, George, 96–97, 99–102

Fortifications at the Manasas (Bull Run) Battlefield, 28, 61

Fry, Roger, 12

Gandhi, 74

Galbraith, Peter, 57

Gardner, Alexander, 60, 61

Gautherot, Claude, 60

Geneva Convention, 21

Gettysburg Battlefield, 60

Giles, Lionel, 77

Goldhagen, Daniel, 87

Gombrich, Ernst, 12

Goya, Francisco, 45, 60, 70–71

Greatest Generation. *See* World War II

Greenberg, Clement, 11; as gatekeeper, 12; on kitsch, 4–5

Haass, Richard, vii, 57

Hanson, Norwood Russell, 73

Hart, Gary, 103

Heraclitus, vii

Heymann, Philip, 95

Hitler, Adolf, 18, 88

Hosterey, Ingeborg, 12

Hussien, Saddam, 64

Incidents of War: The Harvest of Death, 29, 60–61

Infantry Using Flamethrowers, 31, 61

International System of Typographical Picture Education, 14, 87

Internet, 82, 108–109

Isreali-Palestinian Conflict, 40–41, 65, 72, 86

Iraq War Amputee in College, 38, 64

Iraq Wars, 20–21, 38–39, 42, 57, 64–65, 72

I Want You for U.S. Army, 31, 48, 61–62, 87

Jorgensen, Victor, 62
jus ad bellum. See just war theory
jus in bello. See just war theory
just war. *See* just war theory
just war theory, 18–21, 54, 84, 95

kamikaze, 83, 94
Kant, Immanuel, xiv, 3, 21, 97;
    sublime aesthetics of, 6–9
Keller, Simon, 95
Kelly, Captain Colin, 81–82
Kissing the War Goodbye, 32, 62,
    103
kitsch. *See* avant-garde
Koestler, Arthur, 80
Kolb, Robert, 18

bin Laden, Osama, 63
LeShan, Lawrence, 79–80, 82–83,
    85, 88
Lin, Maya, 63
Lyotard, Jean-François, 11, 18;
    postmodern aesthetics of, 6–9

Machiavelli, Niccolo, 77–78
Magritte, René, 49, 62
Manassas (Bull Run) Battlefield,
    28, 60
Margalit, Avishai, 85–86
Marshall Plan, 50
modern art. *See* art
modernism, 3. *See also* aesthetics
Moseley, Alexander, 18, 22

Napoleon at the Battle of Ratisbon,
    27, 60
Napoleon, Bonaparte, 43–44, 59–
    60, 71, 74

Napoleon Crossing St. Bernard, 26,
    59
Napoleonic code, 44
Napoleanic Wars, *26–27,* 43–45, 50,
    59–60, 70
Neurath, Otto, 14
Nietzsche, Friedrich, 69–71, 75

Obama, Barack, 91
O'Keeffe, Georgia, 10–11
Olin, Jens David, 96–97, 99–102
Over the Top, 30, 61

Palestinian Suicide Bomber, 41, 65
Parliamentary Recruitment
    Committee, 49
Pearl Harbor, 21
photographic reality, 69–70, 75, 81
political-revolutionary art, 2
postmodernism: cultural
    complexity of, xii. *See also*
    aesthetics; war images
Powell, Colin, 102
pragmatists. *See* American
    pragmatists
psychology of war. *See* war

Riefenstahl, Leni, 18
Rockwell, Norman, 14
Rosie the Riveter, 51
Rousseau, Jean-Jacques, 20

Saddam Hussein Statue Toppled in
    Baghdad, 39, 64
Santa Fe: art culture of, 10–11
self-censorship. *See* censorship
Smart Bombing of Baghdag, 38, 64
Smith, Adam, 3

Stewart, Potter, 90
the Sublime. *See* aesthetics

Taliban, 55–56
Taliban Fighters, 37, 56, 64
Tel Aviv: Suicide Bombing
Aftermath, 41, 59, 65
Ten Commandments, 19
terrorism. *See* war
theory of war. *See* war
Third of May, 27, 60
Twitter, 1
Twin Towers. *See* World Trade
Center Twin Towers
Tzu, Sun, 76–79

United Nations Charter, 97–98
United Nations Security Council,
97
United States of America Civil War,
xii, *28–29,* 45–47, 50, 54, 60–61,
72, 81
U.S. 1st Calvary Division
(Airmobile), 34, 63

Viet Cong, 54, 63
Vietnam War, *34–35,* 49, 53–56,
63, 68
Vietnam War Veterans' Memorial,
34, 63
von Clausewitz, Carl, vii, 59, 75–79

Walzer, Michael, 22, 84–86, 89,
94–97
war, vii–viii, 23, 42–43, 67–68;
causes of, 79–80; legality of,
95–99; legitimate defense, 97,
99–101; moral conduct of, 21–
23, 74–75, 84–86, 99–100; moral

perspectives on, 80–81, 84–85,
104; psychology of, 79–82; and
terrorism, 93–95; theory of, 75–
79; underlying motivations for,
82–83. *See also* Just War Theory

war images: considerations for
analysis, 42–43; consumption
of, 14–15; cultural importance
of, vii–ix, 14; distribution of, 2,
14; fabrication of reality, x–xi,
15, 45–46, 75, 102; ideology of,
x, 13; image groupings, 25–41;
interpretation of, viii, xii, 15–17,
45, 68, 106–108; interpretive
manipulation, 18, 68; modernist,
69–71; pragmatic reading of,
x, 23–24, 45; postmodernist,
69–71; problems of representing
reality, 69–75; selective truth
of, 15. *See also* aesthetics;
censorship; critical engagement;
photographic reality
War of the Greatest Generation.
See World War II
War on Terror, 94
Waud, Alfred, 60
weapons of mass destruction, 19,
57, 102
West Bank, 59, 65
West Bank Security Barrier, 40, 65
Wikipedia, 108
Wittgenstein, Ludwig, 14
World Trade Center Attacked, 36, 63
World Trade Center Twin Towers,
55, 63, 94
World War I, 48–51, 55, 61–62
World War II, 50–53, 55, 62, 73, 87,
100, 103

ABOUT THE AUTHORS

Raphael Sassower is professor of philosophy at the University of Colorado, Colorado Springs. His latest books include *Postcapitalism: Moving Beyond Ideology in Economic Crises* (2009), *Ethical Choices in Contemporary Medicine*, with Mary Ann Cutter (2007), *Popper's Legacy: Rethinking Politics, Economics, and Science* (2006), and *Political Blind Spots: Reading the Ideology of Images*, with Louis Cicotello (2006).

Louis Cicotello is Professor Emeritus of Visual Art at the University of Colorado, Colorado Springs. In addition to collaborating with Raphael Sassower on *The Golden Avant-garde* and *Political Blind Spots* he has exhibited his artwork nationwide and designed theatrical sets, most recently for the Colorado Opera Company. The collage used on the front cover was created by him.